IMAGES OF V

ARMOURED WARFARE IN THE VIETNAM WAR

RARE PHOTOGRAPHS FROM WARTIME ARCHIVES

Michael Green

Pen & Sword

MILITARY

First published in Great Britain in 2014 by
PEN & SWORD MILITARY
An imprint of
Pen & Sword Books Ltd
47 Church Street
Barnsley
South Yorkshire
S70 2AS

ISBN 978-1-78159-381-3

Typeset by Concept, Huddersfield, West Yorkshire HD4 5JL.
Printed and bound in India by Replika Press Pvt. Ltd.

Pen & Sword Books Ltd incorporates the imprints of Pen & Sword Archaeology, Atlas, Aviation, Battleground, Discovery, Family History, History, Maritime, Military, Naval, Politics, Railways, Select, Social History, Transport, True Crime, and Claymore Press, Frontline Books, Leo Cooper, Praetorian Press, Remember When, Seaforth Publishing and Wharncliffe.

For a complete list of Pen & Sword titles please contact
PEN & SWORD BOOKS LIMITED
47 Church Street, Barnsley, South Yorkshire, S70 2AS, England
E-mail: enquiries@pen-and-sword.co.uk
Website: www.pen-and-sword.co.uk

Contents

Acknowledgments

As with any published work, authors must depend on their friends for assistance. Those who provided valuable support for this book include Jim Mesko, Joe De Marco, Martin Morgan and Vladimir Yakubov. Paul and Lorén Hannah were kind enough to provide access to their wide assortment of military vehicle images taken on their travels across the United States. The pictures from the Tim Kubica collection that came from Thomas F. Meyer were provided by the late Richard Hunnicutt.

A special note of thanks goes to Ken Estes and Michael Panchyshyn for taking the time to review the text and pictures for accuracy.

William Highlander, director of communications for FMC, provided the author permission to access the firm's picture library. Other organizations that assisted the author in acquiring images for this book include the helpful staffs of the former Patton Museum of Armour and Cavalry, the National Archives, and the Tank Museum, Bovington, England. Randy Talbot, the TACOM Life Cycle Management Command (LCMC) staff historian, allowed the author access to their extensive historical photo collection. As the images for this book come from a wide variety of different sources individual picture quality can vary a great deal. Some less than perfect images have been included due to their rarity.

Dedication

I would like to dedicate this book to
tanker Lieutenant Colonel Robert M. Johnstone
(USMC retired).

Foreword

Tanks are not supposed to operate in the jungle. That was the opinion of most of the US Army's leadership in the 1960s. I was a newly-trained second lieutenant in the armour branch in 1969 and was told to forget about being a tanker. Instead, it was conveyed to me that I could expect an assignment as an infantry platoon leader in Vietnam. 'This is an infantry war', I was informed on a number of occasions before flying off to the war zone. I would be leading my men into battle on foot through fetid jungles infested with poisonous snakes and insects, or slogging waist-deep through the mud and muck of a rice paddy. Upon my arrival in Southeast Asia what I found was completely at odds with what I had been told.

Once in South Vietnam I found myself assigned to Troop E, 1st Cavalry of the 11th Light Infantry Brigade of the American Division. Instead of walking into battle I would be riding into harm's way on an aluminium armoured steed dubbed the ACAV. Our escort would be the Sheridan light tank. To my great surprise not all of Vietnam was composed of jungles and rice paddies. A lot of the land was a flat alluvial plain and some areas were rolling hills. Especially during the dry season most of the country was accessible to light armoured vehicles. Even the much heavier M48 Patton tanks were surprisingly mobile in many areas. I found that we could operate pretty much anywhere we chose to go. It turned out that armoured vehicles could operate successfully in Vietnam when employed with imagination and ingenuity.

Of the two vehicles I had under my command in South Vietnam I spent most of my time on the ACAV. I liked its reliability despite the abuse we heaped upon it. To improve our chances of survival when encountering the numerous mines and improvised explosive devices the enemy lay in our path, our vehicles had been supplied with a belly armour kit. We also carried an enormous amount of ammunition. This extra weight placed a serious burden on the vehicles and no doubt shortened their mechanical life spans. But we all wanted to go home in one piece.

I had limited faith in the Sheridans in my platoon. They had too many bugs and too many problems with reliability. Sometimes I wished we had M48 Patton tanks for busting through dense undergrowth in our constant search for the enemy's hideouts. However, when a Sheridan got stuck, you could hook a couple of ACAVs up and pull it out of the mire. You couldn't do this with an M48. As our troop commander said: 'You get an M48 stuck at 52 tons you have a real problem!' So while we gained mobility we lost reliability, firepower and armoured protection.

Another surprise for me upon being asked by the author to write a foreword for this book was to realize the incredible array of armoured vehicles that had served in that region of the world prior to my arrival and during my time in country. I trust that the readers of this book will enjoy this concise look at these vehicles and what they brought to the conflict that plagued that far corner of the world for so long.

Todd Armstrong

Note to readers

The US Army implemented a new system of tank nomenclature in late 1950. No longer were they divided by weight into light, medium or heavy tanks. Rather, they were classified by the calibre of their main guns. As an example, the M48 medium tank was officially referred to in US Army documents after November 1950 as the 90mm gun tank M48A3. To be consistent, the author will retain the original classification of American tanks as being light, medium or heavy throughout the text.

Chapter One

Tanks

At the conclusion of the First World War in 1918, the French military began deploying a small number of FT-17 light tanks to the far reaches of its colonial empire. One such French colony that acquired the light tanks was Indochina. Indochina is an anachronistic term, but at that time encompassed a region that includes the current countries of Cambodia, Laos and Vietnam. The modern name for the former Indochina region is Southeast Asia.

The FT-17 light tank was a two-man vehicle that weighed 15,432lb (7mt) and was powered by a gasoline engine that provided it a top speed of 4.7mph (7.7km/h). The operational range of the vehicle was approximately 22 miles (35km) on level roads. Armament on the FT-17 light tank was either a single 8mm machine-gun or a short-barrel 37mm main gun. Maximum armour thickness on the front of the vehicle was 22mm.

Twenty or so of the French military's FT-17 light tanks survived in Indochina until early 1945. Half were stationed in the northern city of Hanoi and the other half in the southern city of Saigon. Due to the harsh local environmental weather conditions, the vehicles' operational ready rates were extremely low. In a 1936 inspector-general's report it was mentioned that the tanks were only run once a year on France's Independence Day.

The seeds of conflict

The uneasy alliance between Japanese military forces and the French colonial military forces in Indochina that had been in effect since September 1940 came to an abrupt end in March 1945. At this point the Japanese overwhelmed and disarmed the French troops in Vietnam and sent them off to prisoner-of-war camps. The Japanese Army units stationed in Vietnam were assisted by their own tank units, equipped with the Type 95 light tank and the Type 89 medium tank.

The Type 95 light tank was a three-man vehicle that weighed 16,314lb (7.4mt) and was powered by a diesel engine that provided it a top speed of 28mph (45km/h). The operational range of the vehicle was approximately 156 miles (250km) on level roads. Armament on the Type 95 light tank consisted of a 37mm main gun and two 7.7mm

Type 97 machine-guns. The maximum armour thickness on the front of the vehicle was 12mm. The Type-95 light tank entered Japanese Army service in 1935.

The Type 89 medium tank was a four-man vehicle that weighed 25,353lb (11.5mt) and was powered by a gasoline engine in early production units that was later replaced with a diesel engine. The operational range of the vehicle was approximately 100 miles (161km) on level roads. It was armed with a 57mm main gun and two 7.7mm machine-guns. Maximum armour thickness on the front of the Type 89 medium tank was 17mm. The vehicle first entered Japanese Army service in 1931.

With the dropping of two atomic bombs on Japan, the Japanese Government surrendered on 15 August 1945. To prevent Indochina from descending into chaos the Allies quickly deployed British Army Commonwealth units to the southern region of the colony and Nationalist Chinese Army units to the northern region of the colony. These forces were to remain in place until the French military could re-establish a presence in the region.

The First Indochina War

In the northern part of Indochina, the Chinese Nationalist Army units had little interest in preserving the status quo for the returning French military. In the resulting power vacuum, the Communist Viet Minh (League for the Independence of Vietnam) established itself as a dominant military and political force. The Viet Minh had less success in the southern part of Indochina due to the pro-French sympathy of the commander of the British Commonwealth units deployed there.

The first elements of the French Far East Expeditionary Force (CEFEO) landed in Indochina in October 1945 with the goal to retake the region. They brought along with them a small number of American-designed and built M5A1 light tanks. These tanks had been supplied to the Free French Army during the Second World War by the American Government under the Lend-Lease program.

The four-man M5A1 light tank weighed 34,700lb (15.7mt). Power for the vehicle came from two liquid-cooled gasoline engines that gave a top speed of 36mph (57.9km/h) and an operational range of approximately 100 miles (161km) on level roads. Armament consisted of a 37mm main gun and up to three .30 calibre (7.62mm) machine-guns, one being coaxial. The maximum armour thickness on the front of the M5A1 light tank was 51mm.

The M5A1 had been officially nicknamed the Stuart by the British during the Second World War. This was done in honour of J.E.B. Stuart, a famous American Civil War (1861–1865) Confederate cavalry commander. It was the British Army that assigned the names of famous American generals to American tanks and not the US Army, until late in the Second World War and thereafter. The production of the M5A1 light tank had begun for the US Army in November 1943.

There was a tentative agreement reached with the French Government that the Viet Minh could become an autonomous member within the French Union, but this was not to be. In December 1946 fighting broke out between the CEFEO and the Viet Minh in what would become commonly known as the First Indochina War.

With the advantage provided by its armoured fighting vehicles, the CEFEO quickly pushed the Viet Minh out of Indochina's urban areas and into the countryside where the Viet Minh began a guerrilla war. With the region's limited road infrastructure – badly deteriorated during the Second World War – the CEFEO found the bulk of its forces road-bound and easy targets for Viet Minh ambushes and mines.

Lacking a sufficient number of American-supplied tanks to deal with the Viet Minh, the CEFEO pressed into service leftover Japanese tanks. The French military, between 1948 and 1949, also shipped a number of two-man Hotchkiss H-39 light tanks to Indochina. The vehicle had first entered French Army service prior to the German invasion of France in the summer of 1940.

The Hotchkiss H-39 light tank weighed 26,456lb (12mt) and was powered by a gasoline engine that gave it a top speed of 22.5mph (36km/h) and an approximate operational range of 93 miles (150km) on level roads. It was armed with a 37mm main gun and a single coaxial 7.5mm machine-gun. The maximum armour thickness on the front of the Hotchkiss H-39 light tank was 40mm.

The CEFEO also employed redundant turrets from some of its pre-Second World War tanks, such as the H-39 light tank and the Renault R-35 light tank in defensive positions in Indochina. Even the turret of a British Army Crusader tank, armed with a 2-pounder (40mm) main gun, was employed at a CEFEO defensive position outside the city of Hanoi.

More American tanks arrive

The Japanese and French tanks employed post-war by the FEF in Indochina were soon supplemented by additional American tanks, including the five-man M4 series medium tank. The Free French Army had received the diesel-engine M4A2 medium tanks during the Second World War through Lend-Lease. Some of these diesel tanks were later converted to gasoline post-war. The Free French Army was also supplied with the gasoline-engine M4A1 medium tank from US Army stockpiles in Western Europe during the Second World War. Pictorial evidence shows both the M4A1 and M4A2 being used by the FEF in Indochina.

The M4 series medium tanks began rolling off the factory floor in 1942 for the US Army and, later, the US Marine Corps. They were armed with either a 75mm or 76mm main gun, two .30 calibre machine-guns (one being the coaxial) and some-times a single .50 calibre (12.7mm) machine-gun on the turret roof. The maximum armour thickness on the front of the M4 series medium tank was 75mm. Delete

The gasoline-engine-powered M4A1 weighed 66,800lb (30mt), had a top speed of 24mph (39km/h) and an approximate operational range of 120 miles (193km) on level roads. The twin diesel-engine-powered M4A2 had a top speed of 25mph and an approximate operational range of 150 miles (241km) on level roads due to the greater thermal efficiency of diesel fuel.

The M4 series medium tank was officially nick-named the Sherman by the British during the Second World War in honour of famous American Civil War Union general, William Tecumseh Sherman. The American military began using the name Sherman late in the Second World War.

The American-supplied replacements to the CEFEO for their aging inventory of M5A1 light tanks and M4 series medium tanks proved to be the M24 light tank. The four-man vehicle weighed 40,500lb (18mt) and was powered by two gasoline engines that gave it a top speed of 35mph (56km/h) and an operational range of approximately 100 miles (161km) on level roads. The vehicle was armed with a 75mm main gun and two .30 calibre machine-guns (one being the coaxial) and often a single .50 calibre machine-gun mounted on the turret roof. Maximum armour thickness on the front of the M24 light tank was 38mm.

The M24 light tank first entered service with the US Army in Western Europe in December 1944. It was seen by the American tankers as a big improvement over the M5A1 light tank as it fired a very effective high-explosive (HE) round. However, it still lacked an armour-piercing (AP) round for the main gun able to penetrate the frontal armour on late-war German tanks and self-propelled guns. The M24 light tank was officially nick-named the Chaffee in honour of Major General Adna R. Chaffee. He was the first commander of the US Army's Armoured Force formed in July 1940 shortly after the successful German invasion of France in May 1940.

The strangest use of the M24 light tank occurred when the CEFEO had ten of them disassembled and flown into their surrounded military base at Dien Bien Phu piece-by-piece and then re-assembled. They were intended to provide much needed mobile fire support for the troops stationed there. That effort was for naught as the Viet Minh captured the base in May 1954. The French Government had pushed for United States military intervention at Dien Bien Phu but this was not to happen as the American Government decided it might have provoked the outbreak of a Third World War in Europe.

A summary of the CEFEO employment of armour in the First Indochina War appeared in this extract from an American Government publication entitled *Armored Combat in Vietnam*, authored by General Donn A. Starry and published in 1989:

> To the French command, improvised in all resources, fighting with limited equipment over a large area, the employment [of armor] became a perpetual headache. Armored units were fragmented; many small posts had as few as two

or three armored vehicles. Such widespread dispersion prevented the collection or retention of any armor reserves to support overworked infantry battalions. When French armored units took to the field, they were road-bound […] Since armored units were generally assigned to support dismounted infantry, their speed and ability to act independently, an important part of any armored unit's contribution to the battle team, were never used.

The defeat of the CEFEO at Dien Ben Phu proved to be the catalyst for the French military's departure from Indochina by September 1956 and the end of the First Indochina War. On 20 July 1954, the French Government signed the Geneva Accords, which dissolved Indochina and temporarily divided a portion of that region into two countries: North Vietnam overseen by the Viet Minh and South Vietnam ruled by the last Emperor of Vietnam with American support. At the time there was a great fear among many of the United States' military and political elite that if the Viet Minh were not stopped from taking control of South Vietnam other nations in the region could be in danger of falling under communist control – the so-called domino theory.

America becomes more involved

Beginning in 1954, American efforts at stabilizing the military situation in South Vietnam consisted of sending in small numbers of military advisors. Their job was to help prepare the Vietnamese National Army (VNA), formed by the CEFEO in 1949, for combat. The VNA became the Army of the Republic of South Vietnam (ARVN) in December 1955. The Viet Minh became the National Liberation Front (NLF) or Viet Cong (VC) in 1960. The VC operated in South Vietnam under the general guidance of the North Vietnamese Army (NVA), also known as the People's Army of Vietnam (PAVN).

As the number of American military advisors in South Vietnam continued to grow, there appeared a growing consensus that the ARVN armoured units needed a replacement for their aging inventory of M24s. The vehicle chosen in 1965 for that role was the four-man M41A3 light tank named the Walker Bulldog, after US Army Lieutenant General Walton H. Walker of Second World War fame. The American military did not employ the M41A3 during the Vietnam War.

Once the ARVN acquired the M41A3 light tank from the American Government, they removed the engines from the majority of their remaining M24 light tanks and employed them as static pillboxes at various military facilities.

The M41A3 weighed 51,800lb (23.5mt) and was powered by a gasoline engine that gave it a top speed of 45mph (72km/h) and an approximate operational range of 100 miles (161km) on level roads. The vehicle's armament consisted of a 76mm main gun and two machine-guns; a coaxial .30 calibre and a .50 calibre on the turret roof. The M41A3 was popular with ARVN tankers as it was both reliable and simple to maintain, and a vast improvement over its predecessor, the aging M24 light tank. Maximum armour thickness on the front of the tank was 32mm.

Like the M24s, the M41A3s in ARVN service were sometimes nicknamed coup tanks or voting machines by American military and civilian personnel in South Vietnam. This was because they often tended to be employed by one faction or another of the country's military and political elite to overthrow whoever was in power at the time. Hence, the armoured units of the ARVN were often moved around, not based on battlefield considerations but on political considerations. It took until 1968 before American military advisors managed to impart some degree of professionalism into the ARVN armoured force leadership. The equipping of ARVN units with tanks reflected a desire by American military advisors to mould the ARVN into a mini-US Army designed to fight the Warsaw Pact, illustrating how poorly the American advisors understood the growing insurgency at the time.

Initial ARVN employment of the M41A3 was not positive as recounted in this passage from an American Government publication entitled *Armoured Combat in Vietnam* by General Donn Starry:

> The fight to save the Plei Me Special Forces Camp [19 to 27 October 1965] allowed American advisers to observe the Vietnamese armored task force in action. Gunnery was poor in the tank units, which were now equipped with M41 tanks. There was no effort to place accurate main gun fire; instead, the Vietnamese tankers shot from the hip in the enemy's general direction and kept firing as fast as possible. Tanks bunched up, and troops demonstrated little aggressiveness, content to stand and fight as in pillboxes. Security was poor; the unit was ambushed on the very first day.

American tankers arrive in South Vietnam

The year 1965 was a critical turning point for American military involvement in what was now referred to as the Vietnam War, or in some quarters as the Second Indochina War. Despite the best efforts of countless American military advisors, the ARVN remained an ineffective fighting force except for a few elite units. The VC had taken advantage of this situation and was becoming an ever-growing threat to the stability of the American-backed South Vietnamese Government. In response, the American Government made a decision to commit its own ground troops to the conflict. The first sent in were the US Marine Corps, who brought with them their M48A3 medium tanks in March 1965. The M48A3 had entered into service with the US Army and US Marine Corps in 1963.

The US Army's senior military commanders in South Vietnam failed to understand how Marine units deployed and were extremely upset with the Marine Corps for bringing along their M48A3s. They believed that tanks were generally unsuitable for the terrain being fought over, the counter-insurgency warfare taking place, and would place an additional burden on the already badly strained logistical support system in the country. As a result of this belief, most of the US Army ground units deployed to South Vietnam in 1965 were forced to leave their M48A3s behind.

The only US Army M48A3-equipped unit deployed to South Vietnam in late 1965 was the 1st Squadron, 4th Cavalry, which formed part of the 1st Infantry Division. Their deployment was authorized by the then chief of staff of the US Army, General Harold K. Johnson, as a test to determine the effectiveness of medium tanks in South Vietnam. Their subsequent success in taking the fight to the enemy opened the gate for the deployment of additional US Army M48A3s to the country the following year.

Patton tank description

The four-man M48A3 was officially named the Patton 48 in honour of General George S. Patton of Second World War fame. However, it was more commonly referred to as just the Patton tank or M48. It became one of the principal armoured fighting vehicles of the Vietnam War and performed everything from convoy escort duties to search and destroy missions.

Lieutenant Colonel Robert Johnstone (USMC retired) recalls the attributes of his M48A3 during his time in South Vietnam:

> While the thick armored hide on our Patton tanks made us immune to mortar fragments and small-arms fire, the RPGs [rocket-propelled grenade launchers] employed by the enemy could penetrate our thickest armor on occasion. Although not every RPG hit would knock out a Patton tank, some of our tanks suffered more than one penetration and continued to function. Typically a penetration that struck a tank's onboard ammunition would often result in its complete destruction and a horrible death to the hapless crew.

The 90mm main gun on the M48A3 fired a very useful HE round, designated the M71A1 HE-T (high explosive-tracer) that could destroy enemy bunkers. It also fired two types of anti-personnel rounds. One of these was designated the M336 canister round, which acted much like an oversize shotgun shell spewing out 1,281 steel pellets in a cone pattern up to 200 yards (183m). The late James Carroll (USMC) recalled that some of the canister projectiles were so old and stiff that they had to soften up their heads with hammer blows before firing them so they would spread out in a pattern when fired.

The other antipersonnel round fired from the 90mm main gun on the M48A3 was designated the M580 APERS-T (anti-personnel-tracer) and contained thousands of metal flechettes (darts). It was nicknamed the bee-hive due to the buzzing sounds the metal flechettes made in flight. Lieutenant Colonel Gene Beerbaum (USMC retired) remembers the corpses of enemy combatants being pinned to the trees after being fired upon by a bee-hive round. The bee-hive round differed from the canister round as it had a time fuse with range settings allowing it to be selectively initiated from the muzzle up to 3,280 yards (3,000m). Both rounds could decimate exposed enemy personnel and were greatly feared by the VC and the NVA.

Marine Corps M48A3 tanks based near the demilitarized zone between South Vietnam and North Vietnam retained tank-killing rounds in their main gun ammunition inventory in case of an intrusion by NVA tanks into South Vietnam. These included an armour-piercing shell with ballistic cap-tracer (APBC-T) round and a high-explosive antitank, shaped charge (HEAT) round.

From a March 1967 US Army report entitled *Mechanized and Combat Operations in Vietnam* appears this statement on the use of canister main gun ammunition:

> The most significant feature of this successful armored task force operation was the fact that the preponderance of kills were made through the use of canister ammunition and machine-gun fire employed at close range. Only rarely were fields of fire adequate for employment of the tank's main armament. Canister ammunition was also employed to knock down foliage and undergrowth concealing enemy locations.

The M48A3 weighed 107,000lb (48.5mt) and was powered by a diesel engine that gave it a top speed of 30mph (48.3km/h) and an approximate operational range of 300 miles (483km) on level roads. The tank was armed with a 90mm main gun and two machine-guns, a coaxial .30 calibre and a .50 calibre machine-gun in a cupola on the turret roof. Maximum armour thickness on the front of the M48A3 was 178mm.

The usefulness of the M48A3 medium tank appears in this extract from a 1974 US Army publication entitled *Vietnam Studies: Tactical and Material Innovations*:

> In December 1966, the 2d Battalion, 34th Armor, was assigned to secure the route from Tay Ninh to Tam, where small groups of Viet Cong had been successfully mining the road. The battalion commander chose to use the 'thunder run' technique to offset this enemy action. During the hours of darkness, a tank company [17 tanks] or platoon [5 tanks] 'ran the road' two or three times at irregular intervals. They fired canister and .50 and 7.62mm machine-guns at likely enemy locations on both sides of the road. After three nights mining incidents stopped, and the first *Chieu Hoi* rallier [defector] surrendered. He attributed his action to the thunder runs. This technique was used by most of the tank units in Vietnam.

Due to a shortage of M48A3s, a number of gasoline-powered M48A2C medium tanks were deployed to South Vietnam by the US Army some time in 1967 and 1968. Because gasoline fuel has less thermal efficiency than diesel fuel, the approximate operational range of the M48A2C was only 160 miles (257km) on level roads. American tankers referred to them as gassers.

In 1971, the ARVN's 20th Armoured Brigade was the first South Vietnamese unit equipped with the American-supplied M48A3. To make sure they took full advantage of the vehicle's capabilities, the unit went through a demanding five-month training program under the watchful eyes of US Army advisors with a special emphasis on gunnery. They put the skills they acquired to good use on Easter Sunday 1 April 1972. On that date, T-54 medium tanks of the NVA's 202d Armoured Regiment attempted to seize a valuable bridge at Dong Ha in South Vietnam under the cover of inclement weather. As a number of NVA tanks rushed the bridge, they came under extremely accurate fire from the ARVN's unit's 44 M48A3s at ranges from 3,062 to 3,500 yards (2,800 to 3,200m). This gunfire quickly dispatched eleven of the NVA tanks and because the NVA commander was unable to identify the source of the long-range fire, he withdrew his unit without firing a round in return.

A new American tank arrives in South Vietnam

In 1969 the US Army shipped to South Vietnam sixty-four M551 Armoured Reconnaissance/Airborne Assault Vehicles (AR/AAV). It was developed for the US Army as a replacement for the M41A3 as that vehicle's 76mm main gun lacked the necessary penetrative power to destroy the Soviet Army's T-54 medium tank.

The M551 weighed 33,460lb (15.2mt), and was powered by a diesel engine that gave it a top speed of 43mph (69km/h) and an approximate operational range of 350 miles (563km) on roads. The armour thickness on the front of the M551 was only proof against .50 calibre machine-gunfire.

Concept studies for the four-man M551 began in 1959 and limited production for the US Army started in 1965. To keep the vehicle's weight down so it could be transported by aircraft, it had an aluminium alloy armour hull and a steel armour turret. The vehicle was officially nicknamed the General Sheridan by the US Army in honour of the Union Civil War general, Philip Sheridan. Most tankers just called it the Sheridan.

The main gun on the M551 was a novel combination gun/missile launcher that could fire a conventional 152mm high-explosive antitank-multi-purpose (HEAT-T-MP) round or a 61.5lb (28kg) infrared-guided antitank missile named the Shillelagh. Unfortunately, the gun/missile system and the combustible propellant case for the conventional ammunition main gun round were plagued by design problems from the start that were never resolved while it was in service. Secondary armament on the tank consisted of two machine-guns, a .50 calibre on the turret roof and a coaxial M73 7.62mm machine-gun. Reflecting the fact that the US Army senior leadership saw little chance of the M551 encountering enemy tanks in South Vietnam, the troublesome antitank missile guidance system was removed from the vehicles shipped to Southeast Asia. The M551 arrived in theatre with its 152mm multi-purpose HEAT-T-MP round as well as a canister and a bee-hive round.

A description of the first use of the bee-hive round in South Vietnam by an M551 appears in an article entitled *A Sheridan Memoir: The Early Days*, that was written by Lieutenant Colonel Burton S. Boudinot (retired) and appeared in the January–February 1997 issue of *Armour* magazine:

> In early January 1969, the first Sheridans and their new equipment training teams arrived in Vietnam. The reception by the 11th Armored Cavalry was cool. Then on January 29, two Sheridan's were on picket duty along the Long Binh highway. At about 0230, the crewmen were alerted of movement to their front. The Sheridan searchlights were turned on, and enemy troops were sighted across a dirt road. Two 152mm rounds were fired, each sending hundreds of small, arrow-like flecettes down range. At daylight, 125 bodies were found, along with dozens of blood trails.

Sadly, the combustible propellant case for the conventional ammunition main gun rounds for the M551 proved more fragile than expected and could easily be damaged by mine blasts or even vehicle vibration. The rounds were also prone to swelling in the heat and humidity of South Vietnam, which meant the rounds were difficult to chamber in the vehicle's main gun and often resulted in misfires.

Only ever intended as a reconnaissance tank, the M551's thin armour made it an extremely unpopular vehicle for many American tankers in the Vietnam War when it was improperly used as a *de facto* replacement for the M48 medium tank. It lacked the heft of the M48A3 and its ability to bust through jungle undergrowth. It also lacked the latter vehicle's thick, well-shaped steel armour hide that made it a much more survivable vehicle for its crews when encountering enemy antitank weapons, such as mines. Colonel Peter D. Wells (US Army retired) recalls:

> I returned to duty with my unit 2nd Platoon, A Troop, 3rd Squadron, 4th Cavalry in February 1969. That same month saw the introduction of the M551 Sheridan armored reconnaissance airborne, as a replacement for the Patton tank [...] Our unit's tankers were not happy about turning in their well-armored, 52-ton [47mt] Patton tanks for the thinly armored Sheridan. They felt naked and exposed in the field on the new light tank. When the first one hit an antitank mine, the hull ruptured, the vehicle caught fire, and then it burned to a pile of slag; this incident further undercut the soldier's confidence in the Sheridan.

Australian tank

The Australian Government, in support of the American military effort in Southeast Asia, eventually sent fifty-eight Centurion Mk 5s to South Vietnam, beginning in 1968.

The tank had entered both British and Australian army service in 1952. It weighed 111,966lb (51mt) and was powered by a gasoline engine that provided a top speed of 21.5mph (34.6km/h). It had a maximum operational range of approximately 62.5 miles (100.6km) on level roads. The Centurion Mk 5 was armed with a 20-pounder (83.4mm) main gun and two .30 machine-guns, one of them a coaxial weapon and the other mounted on the turret roof. Maximum armour thickness on the front of the tank was 152mm.

North Vietnamese Army tanks

The NVA formed its first armoured unit in October 1959 with T-34-85 medium tanks delivered by the Soviet Union. The T-34-85 first appeared in service in 1944 and was the Red Army's answer to the German Panther medium tank and the Tiger E heavy tank. Weighing 70,547lb (32mt) the five-man vehicle was powered by a diesel engine that provided a top speed of 34mph (55km/h) and an approximate operational range of 186 miles (300km) on level roads. The T-34-85 was armed with an 85mm main gun and two 7.62mm machine-guns, one being the coaxial. Maximum armour thickness on the front of the vehicle was 90mm. The T-34-85 was built post-war in the Soviet Union and license-built in Poland and the then-Czechoslovakia.

From the Soviet Union, in the late 1960s, the NVA began receiving the T-54A and T-54B medium tanks, and the PT-76 light amphibious tank. The four-man T-54 series medium tank was the post-war replacement for the T-34-85 medium tank. It weighed 79,366lb (36mt) and was powered by a diesel engine that provided it a top speed of 30mph (48km/h) and an approximate operational range on level roads of 310 miles (500km.) The T-54 and the majority of the NVA tanks and armoured fighting vehicles were not deployed to South Vietnam until the bulk of American military ground forces had departed the country by 1972. The last American armour units were withdrawn from South Vietnam in 1972, with the remaining American combat soldiers departing in March 1973.

The T-54 series medium tank was armed with a 100mm main gun in a hemi-spherical turret, and three machine-guns. These included two 7.62mm machine-guns and a 12.7mm machine-gun on the turret roof. The maximum armour thickness on the front of the tank was 205mm. The T-54 was superseded in 1958 in Soviet Army service by an improved version of the vehicle, designated the T-55 medium tank. It was an NVA T-54 that crashed through the gate of the South Vietnamese Presidential Palace in Saigon on 30 April 1975 that brought the long-running Vietnam War to its bloody conclusion.

The NVA also received the T-59 medium tank, which was a Chinese copy of the Soviet T-54A medium tank. The Australian Army compared a captured NVA T-59 medium tank in the early 1970s to a Soviet-built T-54A medium tank and the only difference between the two vehicles that they could discern was that the Soviet tank had a welded, dovetailed joint where the bottom of the glacis plate joined the nose plate, while the Chinese copy had a plain butt weld.

The three-man PT-76 amphibious tank was a post-war design that first appeared in Soviet Army service in 1952. It weighed 30,864lb (14mt) and was powered by a diesel engine that provided it with a top speed of 27mph (44km/h). In water the vehicle could obtain a top speed of 6mph (10.2km/h). The approximate operational range of the PT-76 amphibious tank on land was 155 miles (250km) and 43 miles (70km) in water.

The PT-76 amphibious tank was armed with a 76mm main gun and a single coaxial 7.62mm machine-gun. Reflecting the need to be as light as possible to be amphibious and its reconnaissance role, the maximum armour thickness on the front of the tank was only 14mm.

The first use of NVA tanks against the American military forces in South Vietnam occurred on the night of 6–7 February 1968. An attacking force composed of NVA regulars and eleven (various sources say nine to thirteen) supporting PT-76 amphibious tanks overran the US Army Special Forces Camp at Lang Vei. This was accomplished despite American air and artillery support. In the ensuing battle, almost all the Green Berets in the camp became casualties, with ten of them killed and three captured. The indigenous Civilian Irregular Group (CIDG), whom the Green Berets had organized to fight the NVA, lost 219 killed and seventy-seven wounded. The NVA claimed to have lost ninety killed and 220 wounded during the capture of the camp. The Green Berets inside Lang Vei accounted for three of the NVA tanks with a 106mm recoilless rifle before the camp fell. Other NVA tanks were destroyed with American shoulder-fired M74 LAW and white phosphorus (WP) grenades.

On the night of 3 March 1969, NVA PT-76 amphibious tanks attacked the US Army Special Forces Camp near Ben Het, South Vietnam – possibly to destroy a battery of M107 self-propelled 175mm artillery pieces. The NVA seemed unaware of the presence of a platoon of five US Army M48A3s. The resulting engagement was the only occasion during the Vietnam War in which American-crewed tanks directly engaged NVA tanks. It resulted in the NVA's quick withdrawal from the battle-field with the loss of two PT-76 amphibious tanks and a single BTR-50PK armoured personnel carrier. Total casualties for the American tank platoon was two killed and two wounded, with minor damage to a single M48A3.

The last tank introduced to the Vietnam War occurred when the People's Republic of China supplied the NVA in 1970 with a modified version of the Russian PT-76 amphibious tank, designated the Type-63. It had an 85mm main gun mounted in cast armour turret and sported a revised hull design to support the weight of the larger gun and turret, whereas the PT-76 had a welded armour turret. Unlike the original Russian PT-76 amphibious tank that had a three-man crew, the Chinese Type-63 had a four-man crew. The vehicle weighed 42,549lb (19.3mt) and was powered by a diesel engine that gave it a top speed of 40mph (64km/h) on roads and 7.4mph (12km/h) in the water. It had an approximate operational range of 230 miles (370km) on level roads and 75 miles (120km) in water. The maximum armour thickness on the Type-63 was 14mm.

The first production unit of the French-designed and built FT-17 light tank rolled off the assembly line in September 1917. It was the first tank to feature a turret that could be traversed 360 degrees. On display at the Parola Tank Museum in Finland is this beautifully restored Renault FT-17 light tank. (*Andreas Kirchhoff*)

(*Above*) Part of the vehicle collection of the Belgian National Military Museum is this restored Renault FT-17 light tank. The vehicle, when fitted with an anti-ditching tail piece, was 16 feet 5 inches long (5m) and had a width of 5 feet 9 inches (1.74m). The height of the tank was 6 feet 7 inches (2.14m).
(*Pierre Olivier-BUAN*)

(*Opposite above*) A Japanese commander guides the driver of his Type 95 light tank into captivity at the end of the Second World War as British Commonwealth soldiers look on. The vehicle was 14 feet 4 inches (4.38m) long and 6 feet 9 inches (2.06m) wide. The Type 95 had a height of 7 feet 2 inches (2.18m). (*Patton Museum*)

(*Opposite below*) Shown here on display at the former US Army Ordnance Museum, which was located at Aberdeen Proving Ground, Maryland, is an unrestored Japanese Army Type 89 medium tank. The tank first saw combat during the Japanese military conquest of a great portion of China. The vehicle was 18 feet 10 inches (5.73m) in length and 7 feet (2.13m) wide. It had a height of 8 feet 5 inches (2.56m). (*Michael Green*)

(*Above*) Pictured is a restored M5A1 light tank. The vehicle's M6 37mm main gun fired two types of armour-piercing (AP) rounds that were of limited use to the CEFEO in Indochina. More useful were the weapon's high-explosive (HE) round and a canister round that contained 122 small steel balls. (*Michael Green*)

(*Opposite above*) The M5A1 light tank shown is in US Army Second World War markings and has foul weather canvas covers fitted over all of its weapons. Length of the vehicle was 15 feet 10.5 inches (4.72m) and width was 7 feet 6 inches (2.32m.) The height of the M5A1 was 8 feet 5 inches (2.6m). (*Pierre Olivier-BUAN*)

(*Opposite below*) Belonging to the collection of the Tank Museum located at Saumur, France is this restored and running example of the Hotchkiss H-39 light tank. When fielded before the Second World War, the vehicle was intended to work either with the French Army Cavalry as a reconnaissance tank or with the infantry as a support tank. (*Christophe Vallier*)

(*Above*) An American-supplied M4A1 medium tank of the CEFEO is shown in support of Vietnamese National Army soldiers. The 75mm main gun on the M4A1 fired a very effective HE round. At the height of its involvement in the First Indochina War, the CEFEO had 452 tanks and tank destroyers operating in Indochina. (*Jim Mesko collection*)

(*Opposite above*) The M4A2 medium tank seen here on display in France as a monument vehicle rode on narrow 16.56 inch (421mm) wide tracks, as did the M4A1 medium tanks. These narrow tracks meant that the cross-country mobility of the vehicles was very poor on soft, muddy ground, something that Indochina had a great deal of during the rainy season. (*Pierre Olivier-BUAN*)

(*Opposite below*) CEFEO tankers man an M24 light tank in Indochina. A total of 4,415 units of the M24 were built between April 1944 and June 1945 in American factories. It was the replacement for the M5A1 light tank and remained in US Army service until 1953. (*Patton Museum*)

(*Above*) On display in France as a monument vehicle is this M24 light tank. One of the biggest problems the CEFEO faced in Indochina with keeping its tanks serviceable was the abysmal logistical system that was in place, which resulted in the delivery of spare parts months after requisitioned. (*Pierre Olivier-BUAN*)

(*Opposite above*) Forming part of the impressive inventory of vehicles at the Tank Museum located at Saumur, France, is this running M24 light tank. The vehicle had an overall length of 18 feet (5.49m) and had a width of 9 feet 8 inches (2.95m.) The vehicle topped out at 8 feet 2 inches (2.77m) high. (*Christophe Vallier*)

(*Opposite below*) With the withdrawal of the last soldiers of the CEFEO from Indochina in 1956, their tanks and other military equipment were left behind to arm the new Army of the Republic of South Vietnam (ARVN). Pictured during a parade in Saigon, the capital of South Vietnam, are some of the M24 light tanks of the ARVN. (*Jim Mesko collection*)

(*Above*) ARVN infantrymen are seen here working in conjunction with one of their M24 light tanks. The ARVN tankers, successor to the Vietnamese Armor Corps in 1950, inherited a mindset that restricted tanks to an almost strictly defensive role. Rather than initiating action, they tended only to react to enemy attacks. (*Jim Mesko collection*)

(*Above*) An ARVN M24 light tank is seen in action. The name Vic Morrow is painted on the side of the turret. He was an American actor that appeared on a long-running television series named *Combat*. That series was shown on the American military television network in the country during the height of the American military involvement in the Vietnam War. (*Jim Mesko collection*)

(*Opposite below*) A US Army M41 series light tank is shown on a firing range in the then West Germany in July 1955. Reflecting the haste in which the vehicle was built, it went through a series of modifications to improve its reliability but there was little to externally identify one version from the other. (*Patton Museum*)

(*Above*) An ARVN M41A3 light tank carrying a number of infantrymen is being directed into position by ground guides. The vehicle had an overall length of 26 feet 11 inches (8.2m) and a width of 10 feet 6 inches (3.2m). To the top of its turret-mounted .50 calibre (12.7mm) machine-gun, the vehicle was 10 feet 1 inch (3.1m) high. (*Jim Mesko collection*)

(*Opposite above*) On display at the now-closed Patton Museum of Armour and Cavalry, located at Fort Knox, Kentucky, is an M41A3 series light tank. Development of the vehicle began in 1946. The fear of a third world war resulted in the US Army having the M41 series rushed into production, with approximately 5,500 units completed. (*Dick Hunnicutt*)

(*Opposite below*) Pictured is a derelict M41A3 light tank stripped for parts on an ARVN base. What led to the tank's demise is difficult to determine but one might suspect mine damage warped the vehicle's chassis. Mines accounted for over 70 per cent of the American and ARVN tanks damaged or destroyed during the Vietnam War. (*Jim Mesko collection*)

(*Above*) An ARVN M41A3 light tank is carrying a length of cyclone fencing on its glacis. This was erected around the front of the vehicle when parked to pre-detonate the warhead from rocket propelled grenade (RPG) launchers. On the top of the vehicle's turret is an identification panel to prevent attack by supporting air assets. The vehicle commander is wearing body armour. (*Jim Mesko collection*)

(*Opposite above*) An ARVN M41A3 light tank is shown in a defensive hull-down position. ARVN armour officers were often loath to commit their tanks to offensive operations that might result in heavy losses in men and equipment. To impart to the young ARVN tank officers the more aggressive use of tanks as practised by the US Army, many received additional training at the US Army Armour School. (*Patton Museum*)

(*Opposite below*) This photograph was taken during an ARVN military ceremony. Notice the addition of sandbags on the turrets of the M41A3 light tanks pictured. This might have offered a measure of stand-off protection from the warheads of enemy antitank weapons such as rocket propelled grenade (RPG) launchers or recoilless rifles. (*Jim Mesko collection*)

(*Above*) The US Army Ordnance Department, in response to complaints about the poor visibility and cramped working environment of the vehicle commander's cupola on the M48A3 medium tank, worked towards a solution to the problem. What was devised was the G305 turret riser seen here that fit under the existing MI cupola and contained nine large laminated vision blocks. (*Patton Museum*)

(*Opposite above*) Pictured are some of the M48A3 medium tanks of B Company, 3rd Marine Tank Battalion onboard a US Navy landing craft heading toward the coast of South Vietnam on 9 March 1965. They were the first American armoured unit deployed to South Vietnam. The remainder of the unit's tanks arrived in-country by July of that same year. (*Patton Museum*)

(*Opposite below*) An M48A3 medium tank of the 3rd Marine Tank Battalion is pictured taking part in Operation Starlight. This two day operation took place in August 1965 and was the first time that Marine Corps tankers entered into battle with the Viet Cong (VC). With the loss of only one tank, and seven damaged, they aided in killing approximately 700 enemy combatants. (*Patton Museum*)

(*Above*) A Marine holds a captured RPG-7 launcher. It fired a shaped-charge warhead that could penetrate up to 12 inches (305mm) of armour plate. The normal engagement range of the weapon was 328 yards (300m) and under. The rocket proved susceptible to cross-winds when in flight that decreased its accuracy. (*Real War Photos*)

(*Opposite above*) M48A3 medium tanks fitted with the G305 turret riser and other improvements were designated the M48A3 (Mod B). A Marine Corps example is seen here during the defence of Khe Sanh in March 1968. Despite the addition of the turret riser, many American tankers in South Vietnam continued to mount machine-guns on top of the M1 cupola as shown here. (*Patton Museum*)

(*Opposite below*) Shown is a Marine Corps M48A3 medium tank during Operation Barren Green, which took place in July 1970. Due to the threat posed by enemy rocket-propelled grenade launchers like the RPG-2 or the more powerful RPG-7, the crews of many M48A3s began adding spare track links to the turrets of their vehicle to act as stand-off armour as seen here. Notice the Marine infantrymen crouching on the tank's rear fenders. (*Jim Mesko collection*)

(*Above*) A Marine Corps M48A3 medium tank is shown guarding a supply column with infantrymen walking point in South Vietnam. The enemy's nuisance-Type mining had a powerful psychological effect on everybody in the field as nobody was ever sure where mines might be located. This slowed down combat operations and forced the American military to clear almost the entire country's road net every day. (*Patton Museum*)

(*Opposite above*) A mine sweeper team checks a narrow country road as the crew of a Marine Corps M48A3 (Mod B) tank awaits the all clear signal. The VC and NVA employed a wide variety of antitank mines, ranging from those supplied by foreign governments to a variety of improvised antitank mines. (*Marine Corps Historical Center*)

(*Opposite below*) An American soldier poses next to an array of captured enemy mines and anti-personnel grenades. Nuisance-Type mining was the most frequent form of antitank warfare practised by the Viet Cong. It involved scattering mines throughout an area rather than well-defined minefields. (*Patton Museum*)

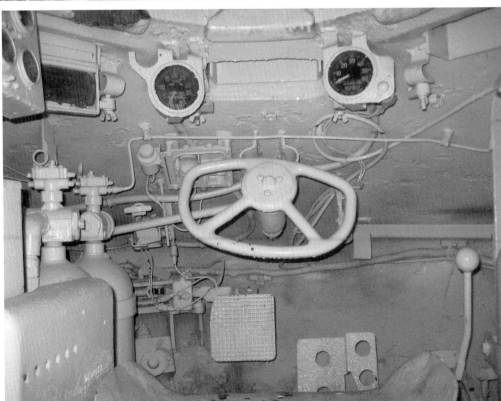

(*Above*) To deal with the large number of mines encountered by American tankers on roadways in South Vietnam, a number of solutions were sought. These included a pressure-Type mine clearance device seen here mounted on the front of an M48A3 (Mod B) medium tank. It was referred to as the ENSURE 202 and met with mixed success. (*Patton Museum*)

(*Opposite above*) Up to its fenders in muck is this US Army M48A3 medium tank. Due to the heat and humidity of South Vietnam, tank crews typically left open their overhead hatches to improve air circulation in their vehicles. In areas of dense vegetation, the enemy took advantage of this habit by getting close enough to the tanks to toss hand grenades down the open hatches. (*Patton Museum*)

(*Opposite below*) Pictured is the driver's compartment of an M48A3 medium tank. Off-road mining by the enemy in South Vietnam caused more damage to armoured vehicles than road mining did. Antitank mines were normally found in their heaviest concentrations around enemy-held positions. (*Chun-Lun Hsu*)

(*Above*) A US Army M48A3 medium is seen speeding down a South Vietnamese road. The turret being reversed seems to indicate the crew has little fear of encountering the enemy. Visible are the vehicle's two large, louvered grill doors hinged at either side of the rear hull that vented the engine exhaust. (*National Archives*)

(*Opposite above*) A Marine Corps M48A3 medium tank that must have just arrived in South Vietnam as it lacks all the creature comforts added by the crews after spending some time in the field, such as field rations, water-proof stowage containers, and improvised armour. Very noticeable in this picture is the vehicle's elliptically-shaped cast armour hull inherited from the M103 heavy tank. (*Patton Museum*)

(*Opposite below*) Mounted on the front of the M48A3 medium tank shown in South Vietnam is the M8A3 bulldozer. The protected hydraulic lines for operating the bulldozer blade ran alongside the upper right hull side of the vehicle. In this image they can be seen fitted over the top of the rear fender mounted air clearer. (*Patton Museum*)

(*Above*) Visible on the front upper hull of this US Army M48A3 medium tank are the hydraulic lines and connections for mounting an M8A3 bulldozer. It was common practice to keep the main gun barrel on the M48A3 tank turned to one side, as seen in this image to avoid the vehicle's driver smashing his head into the bottom side of the barrel when the tank struck a mine. (*Patton Museum*)

(*Opposite above*) ARVN tankers are shown taking a break with their M48A3 (Mod B) medium tanks in April 1972. There was some initial resistance by ARVN tankers to learning the intricacy of the M48A3 rangefinder as insisted on by their American advisors, because the M41A3 light tank they had originally trained on lacked the device. When combat use demonstrated the advantage of rangefinders, the ARVN tankers soon became big fans of the device. (*Patton Museum*)

(*Opposite below*) Pilot vehicle number nine of the XM551 is shown. The production version was known as the M551 Sheridan. The pilot vehicle and early production vehicles can be identified by the thick collar around the rear portion of the barrel. This marked it as a vehicle with an open breech scavenger system. (*TACOM*)

(*Above*) A novel design feature of the M551 Sheridan was a built-in flotation screen, seen here fully erected to enter the water. When not in use, the flotation screen was stored around the perimeter of the vehicle's upper hull. Notice the clear plastic insert in the front of the flotation screen to assist the driver in navigating the tank in and out of the water. (*TACOM*)

(*Opposite above*) A line of newly arrived M551 Sheridan tanks in South Vietnam await assignment. The vehicles pictured are late production units as they do not have the thick collar on their 152mm main gun as seen on early production units. These were fitted with a closed breech scavenger system, which prevented smouldering residue from the previous round entering into the turret. (*Patton Museum*)

(*Opposite below*) This M551 Sheridan in South Vietnam has an RPG screen fitted to the front of the vehicle's hull. RPGs proved to be the biggest threat to the Sheridan tanks that served in Southeast Asia. If an RPG penetrated the turret, it could set off the main gun combustible cartridge cases and result in a catastrophic loss of vehicle and crew. (*Patton Museum*)

Pictured are several M551 Sheridan tanks on a firing range in South Vietnam. The strong recoil forces generated by the firing of the conventional rounds have raised the front of the vehicle off the ground in the centre of the picture. Crew members on the Sheridan were instructed to always brace themselves when firing conventional rounds for fear of injury. (*Patton Museum*)

The M551 Sheridan shown here on patrol in South Vietnam has a front gun shield borrowed from one originally designed for the M113 armoured personnel carrier. The fact that the Sheridan was even deployed for service in South Vietnam was remarkable. Prior testing had concluded that it was unsuitable for use in hot and humid conditions. Reasons included a poorly designed engine cooling system and combustible cartridge case main gun rounds that proved very susceptible to moisture. (*Patton Museum*)

Despite test results that showed the M551 Sheridan was not the preferred candidate for employment in Southeast Asia, the vehicle had enough supporters that wanted to prove the naysayers wrong such that more than 200 eventually served in South Vietnam. Here we see a Sheridan in South Vietnam that has a standardized gun shield kit erected around the vehicle commander's cupola and .50 calibre machine-gun, nicknamed the birdcage. (*Patton Museum*)

The crew of an M551 Sheridan in South Vietnam evaluate the damage to their vehicle after running over a mine. To protect the tank's crew from such encounters, an add-on belly armour kit was developed. Despite the added protection, the crews of the Sheridan would often abandon them as quickly as possible when suffering a mine blast for the fear that the onboard combustible cartridge case main gun rounds would detonate. (*Patton Museum*)

(*Above*) The M551 Sheridan pictured in South Vietnam has a number of locally inspired features. These include the improvised bustle rack attached to the rear of the vehicle's turret and smoke grenades arrayed on the side of the vehicle's turret to allow the vehicle commander to mark his location for air assets. There is also a homemade brush guard in front of the driver's position to protect him from being impaled by dense vegetation when his hatch was open. (*Patton Museum*)

(*Opposite above*) Somewhere in South Vietnam is a halted column of Australian Army Centurion Mk 5 tanks. The deployment of these tanks to South Vietnam was not without some discord. Some in the Australian Government, and even in their own military, felt they could serve no useful purpose, despite the fact that American tanks had already proven their worth in Southeast Asia. (*Patton Museum*)

(*Opposite below*) An Australian Army officer is shown briefing his men in South Vietnam with their Centurion Mk 5 tanks parked behind them. A bulldozer blade can be seen on the second tank in the background. The armoured side skirts seen here on the vehicles did not last long in the field, as mud tended to build up within the suspension system and damage the track fenders and the stowage containers that were located on top of them. (*DOD*)

(*Above*) In the shade of a grove of trees, the crew of an Australian Army Centurion Mk 5 remain vigilant for enemy activity. On this particular vehicle, not only have the front glacis headlights been removed, but also their metal guards. Before being deployed to South Vietnam, some of the Centurion tanks had their glacis up-armoured. (*Patton Museum*)

(*Opposite above*) Pictured is an Australian Army Centurion Mk 5 in South Vietnam. The crew erected a sun screen for protection over the turret roof. On top of the rear of the engine compartment is a bracket for holding a number of water-filled jerry cans. At the rear of the vehicle's hull is a large metal stowage container. (*Patton Museum*)

(*Opposite below*) The Australian Army Centurion Mk 5 in the foreground had its front glacis headlights removed as they did not last long when using the vehicle to push through the dense vegetation of South Vietnam. On either side of the front of the turret are smoke grenade launchers, a feature not seen on the American M48A3 medium tank. In the background appears a Centurion-based bridge launcher and an H-13 light utility helicopter. (*Tank Museum*)

(*Above*) Behind the Australian Army Centurion Mk 5 in the foreground is a Centurion-based armoured recovery vehicle Mk 2, followed by an M113 and then another Centurion Mk 5. The smoke grenade launchers on the turret front of the vehicle proved impractical and were later discarded from all the Australian tanks in South Vietnam. (*Tank Museum*)

(*Opposite above*) Belonging to the military vehicle collection of the Evergreen Aviation and Space Museum, in McMinnville, Oregon, is this T-34-85 medium tank. Sources state that thirty-five of these tanks were supplied to the North Vietnamese Army (NVA) in 1959. As far as can be determined, the NVA used them only as training vehicles. (*Michael Green*)

(*Opposite below*) On display at the former US Army Ordnance Museum is this T-34-85 medium tank. The vehicle had an overall length of 26 feet 6 inches (8.1m) and a width of 9 feet (2.7m). The height of the tank was 8 feet (2.44m). There was authorized storage onboard the T-34-85 for between fifty-five and sixty main gun rounds. (*Michael Green*)

(*Above*) On display at a US Army base in the then-West Germany in the early 1980s is this T-54 medium tank. The key external identifying feature for this vehicle is the circular turret ventilator on the right hand side of the upper turret. This feature disappeared from the follow-on T-55 medium tank series. (*Michael Green*)

(*Opposite page*) Shown on manoeuvres is this Eastern Bloc T-54A medium tank. The vehicle entered service with the Soviet Army in 1949. At that time it was considered the most advanced tank of its type. The ballistic performance of the T-54 main gun was the equal of the 90mm main gun on the American M48A3 medium tank. (*Patton Museum*)

(*Below*) Soviet Army T-54A medium tanks are shown on parade in the early 1960s. These later model production units of the vehicle can be identified by their infra-red searchlights as well as the 12.7mm machine-gun mounted on the roof of the vehicle. Also visible at the end of the main gun barrel is a bore evacuator. (*Patton Museum*)

Captured by the ARVN from the North Vietnamese Army in 1972 is a Chinese-built T-59 medium tank. It was almost an exact copy of the Soviet Army T-54A medium tank. However, it lacked the infra-red searchlights seen on the Soviet Army version or the main gun stabilization system. (*Patton Museum*)

On display at the Military Museum of the Chinese People's Revolution located in Beijing, China is this T-59 medium tank. The vehicle began rolling off the assembly line in 1958. Production continued until the 1980s. The Chinese Government eventually exported approximately 6,000 units of the T-59 and an improved version designated the T-69. (*Paul Hannah*)

Forming part of the military vehicle collection of the Evergreen Aviation and Space Museum, located in McMinnville, Oregon, is this PT-76 light amphibious tank. Reflecting its amphibious characteristics, it has a large boxy boat-like hull and a trim vane located on the lower portion of the vehicle's glacis that is raised in the water. *(Michael Green)*

This photograph shows the restored interior of a PT-76 light amphibious tank turret belonging to the Military Vehicle Technology Foundation in California. The vehicle commander, who also acts as the vehicle's gunner, sits on the left of the gun. His sighting controls are visible in this image. The vehicle's loader sits on the right-hand side of the main gun. *(Michael Green)*

The PT-76 light amphibious tank seen here was propelled in water by two hydro jets. Water for the hydro jets was taken in through inlets at the bottom of the hull or along the rear hull sides and expelled through the two large water jet outlets seen at the rear of the vehicle. Notice the external fuel tanks on the roof of the rear hull. (*Patton Museum*)

Belonging to the vehicle collection of the Military Museum of the Chinese People's Revolution located in Beijing, China, is this Type 63 light amphibious tank. Because it has a more powerful diesel engine than its Soviet PT-76 counterpart, the vehicle had a higher power-to-weight ratio, and hence better performance in the water and off-road. (*Paul Hannah*)

An American soldier inspects a knocked-out Chinese-built Type 63 light amphibious tank employed by the NVA. The vehicle combined a chassis copied from the Soviet Army PT-76 light amphibious tank and the turret from the Chinese Type 62 light tank that was armed with an 85mm main gun. (*Patton Museum*)

Chapter Two

Armoured Personnel Carriers

The Free French Army under Lend-Lease acquired half-tracks that were built in great numbers in American factories during the Second World War. The American military adoption of the half-track was based on the successful German Army employment of the vehicle in Poland, 1939 and France, 1940. Pictorial evidence shows the employment of the M2 half-track car, the M3 half-track personnel carrier, and the M5 half-track personnel carrier with the CEFEO in Indochina in their Groupement Mobiles.

Production of the M2 began for the US Army in the spring of 1941. The M3 was a lengthened version of the M2 that could carry thirteen men in contrast to the ten men on the M2. The M3 also entered production for the US Army in 1941. The M5 was a slightly different version of the M3 built by the American International Harvester Company, beginning in 1942. It was intended strictly for Lend-Lease and not by American military ground forces during the Second World War.

The various half-tracks used by the CEFEO in Indochina weighed between 19,195 and 20,500lb (8–9mt) and were all powered by gasoline engines that gave them a top speed of about 40mph (64km/h) and an approximate operational range of 200 miles (322km). The poor off-road mobility of the half-tracks, a feature much criticized by the US Army in the Second World War, generally restricted them to roads in Indochina, which made them easy targets for Viet Minh mines or ambushes.

Armour thickness on the front of the half-tracks used by the CEFEO in Indochina vehicles topped out at 15.9mm for the M5/M5A1. Armament varied but normally consisted only of .30 and .50 calibre machine-guns. A feature unique to the half-tracks of the CEFEO was a stiff angle-shaped canvas covering over the passenger compartment that acted as sun shield as well as deflecting hand grenades.

American-supplied amphibious tractor

Acquired by the French Army post-war was the American-designed and built Second World War era Landing Vehicle Tracked 4 (LVT4). It was built in both non armoured and armoured versions. Those obtained by the CEFEO in Indochina seem to be the armoured version, based on pictorial evidence, and were generally employed as armoured personnel carriers (APCs). They were employed in the Red River Delta region of northern Indochina. This very wet and flooded region was heavily cultivated and crisscrossed by various waterways with few roads, making it well-suited to the amphibious capabilities of the LVT4.

The LVT4 weighed 36,376lb (16.5mt) and was powered by a gasoline engine that gave it a top speed on roads of 20mph (32km/h) and 7.4mph (12km/h) in water. The approximate operational range of the vehicle on roads was 149 miles (240km), and 50 miles (80km) in the water. The maximum armour protection on the front of the vehicle was 13mm. With a crew of three, the LVT4 could carry up to thirty passengers that entered and left the vehicle through a large, manually-operated ramp located at the rear of the vehicle's hull.

To augment the standard shield-protected machine-gun armament of the LVT4 used by the CEFEO, some were fitted with mortars and recoilless rifles. A few were modified to mount a 40mm Bofors automatic cannon in the rear passenger compartment that was protected by an open-topped shield configuration. Despite the initial tactical surprise gained by the CEFEO in Indochina with the LVT4, the Viet Minh soon adapted to their employment and fielded weapons that could destroy the thin-skinned vehicles.

The American M113 arrives in theatre

As the VC, the replacement for the Viet Minh, grew in strength in the early 1960s and became even bolder in their attacks upon the ineffectual ARVN, American military advisors pleaded for and eventually acquired in the spring of 1962 thirty-two brand new M113 APCs for the ARVN. They were intended as replacements for the ARVN's aging inventory of mostly road-bound half-tracks left behind by the CEFEO when they departed Indochina in 1956. The M113 was fully tracked and amphibious, meaning it could transit areas of South Vietnam that had long been impassable to the ARVN's half-tracks.

An innovative design feature of the M113, designed and built by the American firm of FMC, was its aluminium alloy armoured hull that contrasted with the armoured steel hulls of previous US Army APCs, such as the M75 and M59. The M113 weighed 22,900lb (10.4mt) and was powered by a gasoline engine that provided it a top speed of 40mph (64.3km/h) and an approximate operational range of 200 miles (322km) on level roads. It carried a crew of two, plus eleven infantrymen that entered and left the vehicle through a large, hydraulically powered rear hull ramp.

Armament on the M113 consisted of an unprotected, cupola-mounted .50 calibre machine-gun on the vehicle's roof operated by the vehicle commander. The onboard infantrymen could also use their own weapons by opening a roof-mounted overhead hatch, located over the passenger compartment and firing over the sides and rear of their vehicle. However, this was at the expense of exposing themselves to enemy fire.

The first batch of M113 APCs were assigned to ARVN mechanized rifle companies (later referred to as mechanized rifle squadrons) engaged in fighting the VC in the Mekong Delta region of South Vietnam. The area was inundated by water most of the year. It had few roads and those that passed through the area were easily interdicted by the enemy when they chose to do so. The amphibious abilities of the M113 allowed the ARVN to approach VC-controlled areas from unexpected directions, making it more difficult for the enemy to anticipate ARVN offensive operations.

From a US Army report dated January 1963 and entitled *Lessons Learned Number 26 – M113 Operations* comes this description of what the M113 brought to the ARVN in battle:

> In a typical successful use of a mechanized unit in the Delta, the climax is achieved when several M113s close on a sizeable concentration of VC. The VC are killed by fire or are crushed under the tracks as carriers attack at maximum cross-country speed, often ten or fifteen miles per hour [16–24km/h] through water three feet deep [91cm] in hard-bottom paddies. The VC either attempt to evade with the limited mobility of sampans or foot, turn to fight, or hide in sight. Only after as many as possible of those have been shot, crushed, or captured, should riflemen be dismounted from the carriers [M113s] for final mopping up.

An important issue of doctrine on how to employ the M113 in South Vietnam was resolved by the ARVN. They quickly discarded the US Army doctrine that saw the M113 only as a battlefield taxi. The ARVN decided it made more sense to employ it as a tank-like vehicle. To better suit this new role, the ARVN added improvised gun shields, beginning in 1963, to protect the gunners for the M113's cupola-mounted .50 calibre machine-guns. By the following year, the ARVN had a standardized gun shield for the .50 calibre gunner on their ever-increasing numbers of M113s. The ARVN, in contrast to the US Army, did not have the vehicle commander operate the roof-mounted .50 calibre machine-gun on the M113.

To supplement the firepower of their M113s, the ARVN began mounting .30-06 calibre Browning Automatic Rifles (BARs) on either side of the roof-mounted overhead hatch for the troops within to operate. Some were protected by sandbag parapets while others were protected by steel gun shields. The ARVN also adopted for some of their M113s an American-designed and built one-man turret, designated the M74C. It mounted two Browning .30 calibre machine-guns. Additional weapons mounted on ARVN M113s sometimes included varying sizes of recoilless rifles.

From an article by Major Servetus T. Ashworth III entitled *Armor Can Operate in the Delta* that appeared in the March-April 1967 issue of *Armor* magazine appears this description of the maintenance difficulties experienced by the ARVN-equipped M113 units operating in the Mekong Delta:

A continuous 24 hour a day requirement' is the only way to describe main-tenance in this environment. As a result of the constant cross-country move-ment with the suspension system submerged in mud, together with numerous salt water canal crossings, all parts with rubber components have a short life […] Weapons must be continually oiled to protect them against the moisture. Communication equipment should be aired in the sun at every opportunity.

Among the many types of vehicles pressed into service first by the CEFEO and then by the ARVN, as an APC, was an open-topped Canadian-designed and built armoured truck, designated the C15TA. It was a Second World War-era vehicle and was powered by a gasoline engine that gave it a top speed of 40mph (65km/h) and an approximate operational range on level roads of 300 miles (483km). Normally armed with a variety of machine-guns, the maximum armour protection on the front of the 9,920lb (4.5mt) vehicle was 14mm.

The M113 in American use in Vietnam

The US Army began using the M113 in South Vietnam in 1966, four years after the ARVN. They soon began providing the vehicle commander, operating the cupola-mounted .50 calibre machine-gun, with improvised gun shields. Eventually a standard version, made on Okinawa, was introduced. It consisted of a five-sided open-topped armoured box. There was no forward-facing gun shield on the front of the box as the pintle mount for the .50 calibre machine-gun extended out the front of it.

When the 11th Armored Cavalry Regiment deployed to South Vietnam in 1966, their M113s were already equipped with a gun shield kit, dubbed the Model A, designed and built by FMC. US Army documents refer to it as the Type A armament sub-system. Placed upon the standard cupola for the M113 was an open-topped circular armour turret tub, sometimes referred to as the teapot or bathtub, which included a forward-facing gun shield that extended far enough out front to enclose the pintle mount for the .50 calibre machine-gun.

In addition, the Model A gun shield kit included two offset shield-protected M60 (7.62mm) machine-guns mounted on pintles, one on either side of the rear hull roof. There were also provisions to mount a shield or non-shield protected pintle on the M113's opened overhead hull roof hatch for one of the vehicle's authorized M60 machine-guns, if the need developed.

M113s with the Model A gun shield kit were referred to as the armoured cavalry assault vehicle (ACAV) by the men of the 11th Armored Cavalry Regiment. This name was sometimes adopted by other US Army cavalry units fighting in South Vietnam. Eventually, the Model A gun shield kit was applied to almost every US Army M113 in South Vietnam. The M113s, not in cavalry units but that had the Model A gun shield kit, were not referred to as ACAVs, but as tracks.

A new role for the M113 in Vietnam

As the ACAV was no longer just an APC but a tank-like fighting vehicle in cavalry units, there were no longer passengers carried onboard the vehicles, just crewmen. Lieutenant Todd Armstrong of Troop E, 1st Cavalry of the 11th Light Infantry Brigade of the American Division recalls the crew arrangement on the ACAVs within his cavalry unit in 1970 and 1971:

> Our typical ACAV had a crew of four men; the vehicle commander who operated the .50 calibre machine-gun, the driver, and the two guys who rode in the rear of the vehicle and operated the M60 machine-guns. Due to constant personnel shortages we often had as little as three guys on the ACAVs. When the tactical situation called for it, it fell upon the two machine-gunners in the rear of the vehicle to dismount and walk on foot into battle.

Pictorial evidence shows many ACAVs with four-man crews. Some photographs show a fifth man on the vehicles. A diagram in a March 1967 US Army report entitled *Mechanized and Combat Operations in Vietnam* shows the fifth man on ACAVs being labelled as an M79 grenadier. The M79 was a single-shot shoulder-fired 40mm grenade launcher. Some internet sources describe this fifth man onboard ACAVs, or in some cases even a sixth man, as being ammunition handlers. A typical ACAV might carry as many as 2,000 rounds or more of .50 calibre machine-gun ammunition. In addition, it would carry 4,000 rounds or more of 7.62 × 51mm machine-gun ammunition, and forty-eight or more of the 40mm grenades for the M79 grenade launcher. In most cases, additional 5.56mm ammunition for the M-16 was stored in the vehicle.

In a 1974 US Army publication entitled *Vietnam Studies: Tactical and Material Innovations,* this passage explained how the ACAVs responded to enemy ambushes:

> The shock of the initial enemy volley had to be countered with a withering blast of return fire even more shocking to the enemy soldiers. The 11th Armored Cavalry's counter-ambush training emphasized that gunners on odd-numbered vehicles were to fire to the left, those on even numbered vehicles were to fire to the right. If there were no visible targets to engage, the .50 calibre gunners on the armored cavalry assault vehicles (ACAVs) were to begin raking fire at 50 meters [55 yards] and the M60 gunners at 25 meters [27 yards], and the men acting as grenadiers were to start heaving grenades over the sides of the vehicles. The ACAVs carried enough ammunition for about 10 minutes of almost continuous firing.

Many US Army units experimented with various armament arrangements on their M113s during the Vietnam War to increase their firepower, as had the ARVN. This included replacing one of the two shield-protected M60 machine-guns with the Model A gun shield kit and an additional .50 calibre machine-gun or recoilless rifle. Sometimes the crew of an M113 would mount a 7.62mm Gatling-type mini-gun on their vehicles in place of the vehicle commander's cupola-mounted .50 calibre machine-gun. A 40mm automatic grenade launcher could also be mounted in lieu of the standard cupola-mounted .50 calibre machine-gun.

From a March 1967 US Army report entitled *Mechanized and Combat Operations in Vietnam* appears this passage regarding the crew positions on tanks and the M113:

> Tanks and M113s usually operate with all hatches open until contact is made with the enemy. Exposed armor crewmen habitually wear body armor for protection against small arms fire and shell fragments. When moving through dense jungle where claymore mines and booby traps suspended in vines or trees can be expected, squad leaders may require personnel to ride buttoned up inside the M113; when moving on roads or trails through less dense areas where the major threat is from RPG-2 grenades, recoilless rifles and antitank mines, scout and rifle squad members may travel at least partially outside of the vehicle. Those not manning vehicular weapons ride on top of the M113. Upon establishing enemy contact, all take partial cover within the M113; exterior machine-guns continue to be manned; and all personnel who can, occupy firing positions from which they employ their individual weapons against the enemy.

Even before the first production gasoline-engine powered M113 rolled off the production lines in 1960, the US Army was considering installing a more fuel efficient diesel engine in the vehicle. An added benefit with the use of diesel fuel was that it was far less flammable than gasoline, thereby making the M113 much more survivable.

The first production M113 fitted with a diesel engine came off the production lines in 1964; reflecting that change and other improvements to the vehicle's design, it was designated the M113A1. There are no external differences between the M113 and the M113A1.

It took until 1968 before the entire M113 inventory in South Vietnam was switched over to the slightly heavier M113A1 version. Production of the M113A1 continued until 1979 when it was superseded by another improved version, designated the M113A2.

Marine Corps armoured personnel carrier

When the US Marine Corps arrived in South Vietnam, they brought with them the very large and box-like Landing Vehicle Tracked, Personnel 5A1 (LVTP5A1). Often referred to as an amtrac, short for amphibious tractor, the LVTP5 first came off the production lines in 1952 as a replacement for the aging LVT3 introduced into service during the Second World War. A modified LVT3 was the only Second World War amphibious tractor retained by the US Marine Corps post-war.

The steel-clad LVTP5A1 used in South Vietnam weighèd 87,780lb (40mt). It was powered by a gasoline engine that gave it a top speed of 30mph (48km/h) on roads and 6.8mph (11km/h) in water. The approximate operational range of the LVTP5A1 was 190 miles (306km) on level roads and 57 miles (92km) in water. Armed only with a Browning .30 calibre machine-gun in a small, one-man turret, the vehicle had a crew of three men and could carry thirty-four passengers. Maximum armour protection on the front of the vehicle was 6.4mm.

Originally employed by the US Marine Corps in South Vietnam as a much larger cousin of the US Army's M113 APC, the location of the LVTP5A1's fuel tanks at the bottom of the hull meant it was very susceptible to enemy mines. In such situations, the vehicle was normally a complete loss with heavy casualties to those riding within or on top. The LVTP5A1 was soon restricted to logistical resupply runs that minimized its exposure to enemy weapons.

Australian armoured personnel carrier

Australian Army armoured units deployed to South Vietnam brought along with them the M113A1. Originally armed with an unprotected .50 calibre machine-gun, the machine-gun was soon protected by a gun shield fabricated locally. At some point a decision was made to replace the majority of the .50 calibre machine-guns on the Australian Army M113A1s with an American-designed and built one-man turret. The first model was the same the ARVN had adopted for some of their M113s, designated the M74C. It was armed with two Browning .30 calibre machine-guns. The second model one-man turret was designated the T-50 and came from the designers of the American firm of Cadillac Gage. It was armed with a .50 calibre machine-gun and a coaxial .30 calibre machine-gun.

North Vietnamese Army armoured personnel carriers

From the massive stockpiles of the Soviet Union and later the Republic of China, the NVA received a number of APCs in the mid-1960s to match what the American government was supplying the ARVN. These included both wheeled and tracked versions. Wheeled APCs were the Soviet-designed and built BTR-152, BTR-40 and the BTR-60PB. Tracked APCs included the Soviet-designed and built BTR-50PK and the Chinese-designed and built Type-63.

The BTR-152 and BTR-40 APCs were both simple open-topped vehicles. The BTR-152 first appeared in service with the Soviet Army in 1950 and the BTR-40 the following year. In contrast to the M113, neither vehicle was amphibious. The larger BTR-152 weighed 19,621lb (8.9mt) and rode on six wheels. It was powered by a gasoline engine, which gave it a top speed of 40mph (65km/h) and an approximate operational range of 403 miles (650km) on level roads. It had a crew of two and could carry up to seventeen or eighteen passengers. Maximum armour protection on the front of the vehicle was 12mm.

The smaller BTR-40 weighed 11,684lb (5.3mt) and rode on four wheels. It was powered by a gasoline engine that gave it a top speed of 50mph (80km/h) on land and an approximate operational range of 177 miles (285km) on level roads. The BTR-40 had a crew of two and could carry as many as eight passengers. Besides seeing use as an APC, it was also intended to operate as a reconnaissance vehicle. The NVA adapted the vehicle to mount twin 14.5mm heavy machine-guns in its rear passenger compartment and act as an antiaircraft vehicle. Maximum armour protection on the front of the BTR-40 was 8mm thick. Both the BTR-40 and BTR-152 were normally armed only with 7.62mm machine-guns.

Eventually the BTR-152 and BTR-40 in Soviet Army service were replaced beginning in the 1960s by an amphibious APC that rode on eight wheels, designated the BTR-60P. This was superseded by the improved BTR-60PB model in the Soviet Army, which was the version exported to the NVA. This version weighed 22,707lb (10.3mt) and was powered by a gasoline engine that gave it a top speed of 50mph (80km/h) on land and 6mph (10km/h) in the water. The BTR-60PB had an approximate operational range of 310 mikes (500km) on level roads. The vehicle had a three-man crew and could carry eight passengers. Maximum armour protection on the front of the vehicle was 14mm thick. It was armed with a 14.5mm heavy machine-gun in a one-man turret on the vehicle's roof.

As a complement to the BTR-60PB, the Soviet Army took into service in the 1960s the full-tracked amphibious BTR-50PK that weighed 30,864lb (14mt). It was based on the chassis of the PT-76 amphibious tank and was powered by a diesel engine that gave it a top speed on land of 28mph (260km/h) and 9mph (15km/h) in water. An unknown number of BTR-50PK were sent to the NVA by the Soviets.

The BTR-50PK had an approximate operational range of 161 miles on land (500km). Maximum armour protection on the front of the vehicle was 15mm thick. The BTR-50PK had a crew of two and could carry twenty passengers. Standard armament on the vehicle was typically restricted to a 7.62mm machine-gun.

The amphibious Type-63 APC first entered service with the Red Chinese Army in 1964 and remains in service to this day. It was the first Chinese armoured fighting vehicle not copied from an existing Soviet design. Weighing 27,778lb (12.6mt), the vehicle is powered by a diesel engine that provides it a top speed of 37mph (60km/h) and 4mph (6.4km/h) in water. The Type-63 has an approximate operational range on level roads of 311 miles (500km). It has a two- or three-man crew and can carry thirteen passengers. Armament is normally a roof-mounted 12.7mm machine-gun. The maximum armour protection on the front of the vehicle is 14mm.

Australian Army testing of a captured NVA Type-63 APC in the early 1970s concluded that it was a mechanically simple and robustly built vehicle that was overall fairly reliable. Surprisingly, the Type-63 APC was a better riding vehicle than an M113A1 against which it was compared during testing. This was attributed to the Type-63 APC's larger road wheels.

(*Above*) The half-track personnel carrier M3 was eventually fitted with the M49 ring mount as seen here armed with a .50 calibre machine-gun. In this configuration it became the M3A1. The CEFEO seemed to have dispensed with the machine-gun-armed M49 ring-mount in favour of a sloped fabric covering intended to protect the crew and passengers from the elements and deflect hand grenades. (*Bob Fleming*)

(*Opposite above*) Among the different types of American-designed and built half-tracks used by the CEFEO in Indochina was the half-track car M2 seen here. It had seating for ten men. An improved version with the M49 ring mount on the right front of the vehicle, armed with a .50 calibre machine-gun, was designated the half-track car M2A1. (*TACOM*)

(*Opposite below*) Pictured is a half-track personnel carrier M3. It was essentially a lengthened version of the half-track car M2 that could transport thirteen men. It fulfilled many roles, from ambulance to command vehicle for the US Army and the Free French Army during the Second World War, and no doubt did the same for the CEFEO in Indochina. (*TACOM*)

Intended strictly for export under Lend-Lease during the Second World War was the half-track personnel M5 shown here. Unlike the half-track car M2 and the half-track personnel M3/M3A1 that were built of face-hardened armour, the M5 was built of rolled homogenous armour that resulted in the smooth, rounded corners on the rear compartment of the vehicle, in contrast to the sharp-edged corners seen on the other armoured half-tracks. *(TACOM)*

Posed for the photographer are the crew and passengers of a CEFEO landing vehicle tracked (armoured) mark II (LVT(A)2) in Indochina. The amphibious LVT(A)2 was an American-designed and built vehicle employed by the US Marine Corps and the US Army with great success in the Pacific Theatre of Operation during the Second World War. *(Patton Museum)*

Forming part of the US Marine Corps World War II/Korean LVT Museum, located at Camp Pendleton, California is this landing vehicle tracked (armoured) mark II (LVT(A)2). There was a single armoured front panel for the driver who could prop it open in non-combat situations. When in combat, the driver closed the armoured front panel, using a periscope mounted in his overhead hatch for vision. *(Michael Green)*

The aluminium M113 armoured personnel carrier (APC) seen here on a test track became one of the symbols of the US Army's contribution to the Vietnam War. The vehicle, which received its introduction to combat in that conflict, was designed and built by the American firm of FMC. The same company designed and constructed thousands of amphibious tractors during the Second World War for the American military. *(FMC)*

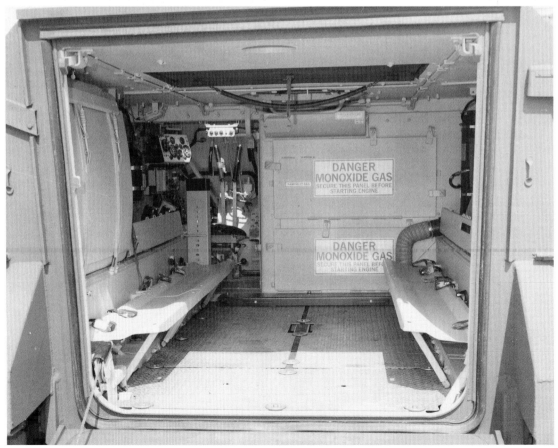

(*Above*) US Army soldiers rush out the rear of M113 APC during a training exercise. When the M113 APC was envisioned it was intended only as a battlefield taxi, a lightly armoured vehicle that could bring into action a squad of infantrymen to provide support to US Army tanks when called upon. Armed only with a single, unprotected .50 calibre (12.7mm) machine-gun it was not supposed to be a fighting vehicle. (*FMC*)

(*Opposite above*) An important design feature of the M113 APC for the US Army was that it was capable of amphibious operations across lakes and rivers without prior preparation. The only things that had to be done prior to entering the water were the extending of a wooden trim vane located at the front of the vehicle's hull and turning on two electric bilge pumps. The M113 was propelled in water by its tracks at approximately 3.5mph (5.633km/h). (*FMC*)

(*Opposite below*) Looking inside an M113 APC, one can see the driver's station at the front of the vehicle's hull on the left-hand side. The engine compartment is located to the right of the driver's station at the front of the hull. Also visible are the two fold-up bench seats on either side of the hull for ten men. Missing from this vehicle is a vertical metal beam in the centre of the troop compartment that supports two seats, one for the squad leader and one for the vehicle commander. (*FMC*)

(*Above*) An ARVN-manned M113 APC is shown after crossing a river. Notice the improvised firing support brackets on the roof of the vehicle for the passengers to rest their personnel weapons at the ready. It was the American Military Advisory Group, in late 1961, which first considered equipping ARVN units deployed to the Mekong Delta region of South Vietnam with the M113 APC. (*Patton Museum*)

(*Opposite above*) Exiting a river somewhere in South Vietnam is an ARVN-manned M113 APC. The seat upon which the crewman who operated the vehicle's roof-mounted .50 calibre machine-gun sat or stood was adjustable in height. (*FMC*)

(*Opposite below*) Being carried on the front of an ARVN-manned M113 APC are three blindfolded Viet Cong prisoners. They are being held in place by the vehicle's lowered wooden trim vane that is rimmed by metal as added support. The VC nicknamed the olive-drab painted, American-supplied M113 APCs, the green dragons. (*FMC*)

The dispirited-looking driver of this ARVN-manned M113 APC is no doubt thinking that he might have misjudged the weight-carrying capacity of the bridge that his vehicle collapsed. As seen here, the ARVN often mounted small, American-designed and built one-man machine-gun-armed turrets on their M113 APCs. *(FMC)*

An ARVN-manned M113 APC enters a waterway at speed. Initial plans called for the M113 APCs being supplied to the ARVN to serve with specially trained rifle companies. This plan soon fell by the wayside and the new ARVN M113 APC units were staffed by a hodge-podge of personnel. This situation led to a poor showing in combat operations until such time that the ARVN officers and men gained some battle experience. *(Patton Museum)*

The armour protection on the M113 APC was designed only to provide a degree of protection from small arms and shell fragments. What happens when the vehicle's protection level was overmatched by an enemy weapon is clearly demonstrated in this picture of an ARVN-manned M113 APC that has suffered a catastrophic internal explosion. (*Patton Museum*)

(*Above*) After overcoming their initial shock on encountering ARVN-equipped M113 APC units, the VC quickly adapted their tactics to deal with this new vehicle. As losses among the crews and passengers in ARVN-manned M113 APCs continued to mount, improvised gun shields, as seen here, began appearing on their vehicles. The vehicle commander in this picture is sitting behind the driver's position. (*Patton Museum*)

(*Opposite above*) This photograph was taken inside an ARVN compound and shows a C15TA armoured truck. Built by General Motors of Canada, the vehicle was modelled on the American-developed and built M3A1 scout car. How many the CEFEO had in service and passed on to the ARVN is unknown. (*Patton Museum*)

(*Opposite below*) As American units equipped with the M113 APC began arriving in South Vietnam in 1965, the wisdom of adding gun shields to the vehicle commander's .50 calibre machine-gun position was apparent to all. Pictured is one of those early improvised gun shield arrangements on a US Army M113 APC. (*Patton Museum*)

To expedite the fielding of gun shields to all the US Army M113 APCs being deployed to South Vietnam, a design was quickly approved and a production line set up on the Japanese island of Okinawa, which was home to a large US Army Ordnance Depot. Pictured is a US Army M113 APC fitted with the new Okinawa gun shield around the vehicle commander's .50 calibre machine-gun. *(Patton Museum)*

The addition of the Okinawa-made gun shield kit did much to cut down the losses among vehicle commanders on US Army M113 APCs, although visibility was greatly limited. As seen in this overhead photograph, the vehicle commander's open hatch provided the rear protection for the gun shield kit. *(Patton Museum)*

The weak spot for the Okinawa-made gun shield kit was the somewhat unprotected frontal quadrant of the arrangement, as is evident in this photograph. Based on pictorial evidence some crews added an improvised shield in front of the Okinawa-made gun shield kit for added protection. *(Patton Museum)*

The soldier in the rear passenger compartment of this US Army M113 APC with the Okinawa-made gun shield kit has built a parapet of sandbags upon the roof of the vehicle upon which to support his 7.62mm M60 machine-gun. The sandbags also provided a measure of protection for the machine-gunner. *(Patton Museum)*

FMC, the designers and builders of the M113 APC, soon stepped up to the plate with a new gun shield kit seen here, referred to in US Army paperwork as the Type A armament sub-system. Besides providing protection for the vehicle commander when operating his .50 calibre machine-gun, there were now gun shields for two 7.62mm M60 machine-gunners in the rear passenger compartment. (*FMC*)

Shown in South Vietnam are two US Army M113 APCs fitted with the Type A armament sub-system. Cavalry units equipped with this weapon and gun shield arrangement on their M113 APCs in Southeast Asia began referring to them as Armored Cavalry Assault Vehicles (ACAVs). Not every M113 APC having the Type A armament sub-system was referred to as an ACAV. (*Patton Museum*)

Looking down into the gun shield for the vehicle commander's position on an M113 APC fitted with the Type A armament sub-system. There were sliding shutters located at the bottom of the vehicle commander's gun shield that lined up with the overhead periscope located in the vehicle commander's cupola. (*FMC*)

Another view of the Type A armament sub-system mounted on an M113 series APC. In this case the vehicle commander's overhead hatch is in the closed position. Notice the close proximity of the vehicle commander's gun shield to the driver's position. The noise and muzzle blast of the weapon being fired directly above his head must have been extremely unpleasant. (*Michael Green*)

Looking down onto the roof of an M113 series APC fitted with the Type A armament sub-system. The gun shields for the two 7.62mm M60 machine-gunners located on either side of the overhead hatch for rear passenger compartment are offset and not directly opposite each other to allow the gunners room to move without bumping in to each other. *(Michael Green)*

An overhead view of the right 7.62mm M60 machine-gun-mount that formed part of a Type A armament sub-system. The M60 machine-gun was first introduced into US Army service in the early 1960s. During its time in use by the American military during the Vietnam War the weapon was not considered as reliable as the much older and more mature design of the .50 calibre machine-gun. *(FMC)*

Shown is the preferred firing position for the machine-gunners in the rear passenger compartment of an M113 series APC fitted with the Type A armament sub-system. To the right of the gunner looking downwards into the vehicle, the squad leader's seat and the vehicle commander's seat can be seen on either side of a vertical metal beam. *(FMC)*

An added feature of the Type A armament sub-system developed and built by FMC for their M113 series APC was a rear-facing pintle mount for an M60 machine-gun as seen here. It was affixed to the bottom of the passenger compartment overhead hatch. Pictorial evidence indicates that it was seldom used in South Vietnam. *(FMC)*

Two M113 series APCs are shown pulling a third vehicle out of a South Vietnamese rice paddy. All three vehicles are equipped with the Type A armament sub-system. The M113 series APC had a torsion bar suspension system with ten individually sprung dual road wheels, five on either side of the vehicle's hull. The steel track shoes were 15 inches wide and had detachable rubber pads. (*Patton Museum*)

Pictured is an M113 series APC fitted with the Type A armament sub-system. The .50 calibre machine-gun that provided the bulk of the vehicle's firepower had an effective range of 2,000 yards (1.83km). In theory, the .50 calibre machine-gun, nicknamed the Ma Deuce or Cal Fifty, has a rate of fire between 450 and 575 rounds per minute. To prevent the barrel from overheating, most machine-gunners fired in short bursts only. (*Patton Museum*)

A posed shot taken during the Vietnam War shows the five-man crew of an ACAV with four armed with the 5.56mm M16A1 rifle. The remaining soldier, referred to as the grenadier, is shown armed with the 40mm M79 grenade launcher. One of the two ACAVs behind the soldiers is armed with an M40 106mm recoilless rifle and associated spotting rifle in place of one of the shield protected 7.62mm M60 machine-guns. *(FMC)*

This photograph is of the same two ACAVs seen in the previous photograph with more details being evident, such as the mounting of a .50 calibre machine-gun in place of one of the shield protected 7.62mm M60 machine-guns. Seen between the two soldiers sitting on the rear roof of the vehicle is a rear-facing, pintle-mounted 7.62mm M60 machine-gun. The cylinders ringing the vehicle commander's position are smoke grenades, to mark the ACAVs position for friendly air assets. *(FMC)*

An M113 series APC is shown in South Vietnam after running over a mine that badly damaged its suspension system. Due to the greater vulnerability of the M113 series APC to enemy mines, it was standard practice to have an M48A3 medium tank lead them into action whenever possible. (*National Archives*)

The damage that a mine could do to the thin, aluminium alloy armoured floor of an M113 series APC is clearly evident in this dramatic photograph. While most M48A3 medium tanks damaged by mines in South Vietnam were repairable, that was not the case with M113 series APC, with many mine-damaged units being total write-offs. (*FMC*)

The crew of an ARVN M113 APC survey the extensive damage to their vehicle after an encounter with an enemy mine. Besides the visible damage to the track and the suspension system, the blast of the explosion dislodged the vehicle commander's gun shield that lies on the ground next to the vehicle. *(National Archives)*

Such was the fear of enemy mines and their effect on the thinly armoured M113 series APCs during the Vietnam War that those who served on the vehicle or rode as passengers spent the majority of their time on the roof of the vehicle, the thought being that a large mine blast would throw them off the vehicle. This was considered a better fate than being trapped inside the vehicle when a mine was encountered. *(National Archives)*

(*Above*) As the drivers of the M113 series APC feared being trapped inside their vehicles when striking an enemy mine, some went to the extreme of having extension rods added to their tiller control levers that allowed them to steer their vehicles from the roof, as is shown here. (*National Archives*)

(*Opposite above*) To deal with the ever-present threat of enemy mines in South Vietnam, the US Army fielded a mine protection kit. It consisted of titanium armour plates welded to the bottom hull of the M113 series APC. To offset the added weight, floatation cells were affixed to the front of the vehicle's hull, as seen here. (*Tim Kubica collection via Thomas F. Meyer*)

(*Opposite below*) An ARVN M113 APC is seen in this picture fitted with the Type A armament sub-system and a flotation cell on its trim vane. There is a beret-wearing US Army advisor on the roof of the vehicle. It appears that the driver of the vehicle has an assortment of hand grenades on the rim of his overhead hatch position for quick use in close combat. (*National Archives*)

US Army soldier Tim Kubica shows off two captured enemy antitank weapons. In his right hand is the launcher unit for the RPG-7. In his left hand is the launcher unit for the older generation RPG-2. The licence-produced version of the RPG-2 built in North Vietnamese factories was referred to as the B-40. (*Tim Kubica collection via Thomas F. Meyer*)

It must have been unnerving for US Army soldiers in the rear of this M113 series APC to view the soldier walking by them with a handful of captured high explosive antitank (HEAT) grenades for the RPG-2. *(Patton Museum)*

Pictured is a US Army M113 series APC fitted with a Type A armament sub-system. It bears a visible hole from an RPG strike and associated spalling on the exterior of the vehicle's hull. The most vulnerable portion of the M113 series APC was the left hull rear corner as that was the location of the vehicle's fuel tank. An RPG strike in this area would often result in a catastrophic fuel fire, especially with the gasoline powered M113 APC. *(Jim Loop via Dick Hunnicutt)*

(*Right*) American tankers in South Vietnam disliked the very cramped M1 vehicle commander's cupola on the M48A3 medium tank armed with a .50 calibre (12.7mm) machine-gun. In its place some units mounted a machine-gun on top of the vehicle commander's cupola as seen on this Marine Corps M48A3. Mounted just in front of the gun shield is a 2.2kw xenon searchlight. (*Robert M. Johnstone*)

(*Below*) Pictured is the bane of existence of every tank crew – getting your vehicle stuck some place that is very difficult to recover from. Despite the perception that South Vietnam's terrain was unsuitable for armoured vehicles like tanks, the US Army discovered that 46 per cent of the country could be traversed by armoured vehicles all year round. (*Patton Museum*)

The off-road environment in South Vietnam took its toll on every aspect of a tank's design. Here we see the crew of an Australian Army Centurion Mk 5 working on one of the drive sprockets of their vehicle. Clearly visible on the tank's main gun barrel is the large, rounded bore evacuator. (*Patton Museum*)

Shown in a South Vietnamese field is an M551 Sheridan belonging to the 3rd Squadron, 4th Cavalry, 25th Infantry Division. The vehicle came with an electric drive control system to traverse the turret and raise and lower the main gun. Unfortunately this feature proved unreliable and caused the greatest number of equipment failures with the vehicle in Southeast Asia. (*Patton Museum*)

As seen here, the soldiers who manned the 7.62mm M60 machine-guns on the US Army M113 APCs deployed to South Vietnam early on lacked any form of armour protection. The gas-operated M60 machine-gun weighed 23.3lb (10.57kg) without its tripod and had a maximum rate of fire of 650 rounds per minute. This rate of fire was seldom used as it would quickly burn out the weapon's barrel in battle. *(National Archives)*

An M113 APC fitted with the Type A armament subsystem is shown on the move in South Vietnam. The vehicle could climb a 60 per cent gradient and cross a trench 5 feet 6 inches (1.68m) wide. It could also climb over vertical walls 24 inches (61cm) high. The M113 APC was 18 feet 4 inches (5.61m) in length and 8 feet 6 inches (2.6m) high, with the .50 calibre machine-gun fitted. Vehicle width was 10 feet seven inches (3.26m). *(National Archives)*

(*Left*) The American soldier pictured manning a shield-protected 7.62mm machine-gun on an M113 series APC in South Vietnam is wearing an armoured vest developed during the Korean War (1950–1953). The heavy and bulky armoured vest proved extremely uncomfortable in the hot and humid temperature of South Vietnam but saved countless lives. (*National Archives*)

(*Below*) Pictured in South Vietnam is this US Army twin 40mm self-propelled gun M42A1, popularly known as the Duster. The gun mount was located in the front centre of the vehicle's hull with 360 degrees of traverse. The power-operated twin 40mm guns could be raised to 85 degrees and lowered to minus 3 degrees. If the hydraulically-power-operated system went down the guns could still be operated manually. (*National Archives*)

Somewhere in South Vietnam an M50A1 Ontos crewman loads one of his vehicle's six M40A1C 106mm recoilless rifles. The need to reload these weapons from outside the vehicle was a serious battlefield drawback. The maximum range of the recoilless rifles on the Ontos firing the APERS-T (anti-personnel-tracer) M581 round, which contained 9,500 flechettes, was 3,600 yards (3,300m). (*National Archives*)

The M49 105mm howitzer in the US Marine Corps LVTH6 shown here in South Vietnam had a coaxial .30 calibre machine-gun fitted for which the vehicle carried 2,000 rounds. The LVTH6 turret could be traversed manually or hydraulically. It had a maximum traverse rate of 360 degrees in seventeen seconds. The turret-mounted weapons could only be elevated and depressed manually. (*National Archives*)

(*Left*) A US Army M30 107mm (4.2 inch) self-propelled mortar carrier M106 or M106A1 in South Vietnam just before the moment of firing. The M30 107mm mortar is rifled and has a maximum range of 4,400 yards (4,023m). It was replaced in American military service in the 1990s by a NATO standard 120mm mortar, designated the M120/M121. (*National Archives*)

(*Below*) Also employed by the US Army during the Vietnam War was the 8 inch self-propelled howitzer M110 seen here. It was mounted on the same chassis as the 175mm self-propelled gun M107 with the weapons being interchangeable using the same gun mount. The barrel on the M110 was 17 feet 10 inches (5.21m) and weighed 8,490 pounds (3,850kg). It could fire a 229 pound (104kg) high explosive round out to a maximum range of 18,373 yards (16,800m). (*National Archives*)

(*Right*) A Marginal Terrain Assault Bridge based on the M113 series vehicle is shown here in South Vietnam. According to one reference source, twenty-nine units were assembled and twenty-five were eventually deployed to Southeast Asia. The bridge could be launched and emplaced in less than two minutes without any personnel being exposed to enemy fire. (*National Archives*)

(*Below*) The crew of a US Army medium recovery vehicle M88 are shown removing the radiator from an M113 APC with the aid of the A frame hoisting boom located on the front roof of the vehicle. The crew's work is being observed by some ARVN tankers with their black berets. The vehicle's roof-mounted .50 calibre machine-gun was operated by the vehicle commander. (*National Archives*)

The logistical lifeblood of the majority of American military bases in South Vietnam were truck convoys. These became a primary target for the enemy and were constantly subjected to ambushes. To protect themselves, the truckers began armouring and arming some of their trucks, as seen here with an M35 2½ ton series cargo truck, nicknamed the Sopwith Camel. (*National Archives*)

The M55 quad machine-gun turret shown here was originally trailer-mounted for use by US Army artillery air defence machine-gun batteries. However, in South Vietnam they were typically mounted on the rear cargo decks of M35 2½ ton series trucks for added mobility as seen here. (*National Archives*)

(*Above*) For ease of engine accessibility, a large portion of the upper front hull of the M113 series APC could be swung upwards, as is seen in this picture. The original M113 was powered by a liquid-cooled gasoline engine, referred to as the Chrysler 75M, which developed 209 horsepower. The later M113A1 was powered by a liquid-cooled diesel engine referred to as the Detroit Diesel 6V53. *Tim Kubica collection via Thomas F. Meyer)*

(*Opposite above*) A somewhat worse-for-wear M113 series APC is shown at a destroyed vehicle collection point in South Vietnam. The reason for its demise is unclear. At this point the vehicle would be evaluated to see if it could be rebuilt or stripped for parts. If it was determined that the vehicle could be rebuilt it would be returned to the FMC factory in the United States. *(FMC)*

(*Opposite below*) To deal with the continued problem posed by the enemy's widespread employment of RPGs during the Vietnam War, many solutions were sought for the M113 series APC. The most elaborate of these was a factory effort seen here that resulted in what is now commonly referred to as bar armour or slat armour. The purpose of the stand-off armour arrangement was to disable or pre-detonate the rocket warheads before impacting with the actual vehicle's hull. *(FMC)*

Pictured are two US Army M113 series APCs supporting US Army infantrymen who are carrying a wounded comrade to safety. The vehicle in the foreground appears to have a M20 75mm recoilless rifle mounted in place of the vehicle commander's .50 calibre machine-gun. Instead of the shield protected 7.62mm M60 machine-gun on the right side of the vehicle there is a .50 calibre machine-gun. (*National Archives*)

The crews of US Army M113 series APCs never stopped trying to improve the firepower of their vehicles. Here we see the replacement of the .50 calibre machine-gun at the vehicle commander's station on an M113 series APC with a US Navy experimental Honeywell Mk 18 40mm grenade launcher. The weapon was fired by turning a hand crank. (*Patton Museum*)

An interesting array of weaponry is seen on this M113 series APC. In place of the vehicle commander's .50 calibre machine-gun is an electrically-powered M134 7.62mm minigun. Mounted on a tall pedestal on the right hand side of the vehicle's rear hull is a 7.62mm M60D machine-gun with spade grips usually used by helicopter door gunners in Vietnam, rather than the standard trigger assembly mounted under the weapon's receiver, as seen on the 7.62mm M60 machine-gun located on the left side of the vehicle. (*Tim Kubica collection via Thomas F. Meyer*)

The death-dealing end of the M134 7.62mm minigun is seen here on the M113 series APC shown in the previous photograph. The gunner on the electrically-powered weapon threw an arming switch to energize the rear hand grips that mount the weapon's two triggers. One trigger starts firing the gun at 2,000 rounds per minute, pressing the second trigger increases the firing rate to 4,000 rounds per minute.

(*Tim Kubica collection via Thomas F. Meyer*)

(*Above*) An M113 series APC with the Type A armament sub-system belonging to the 9th Infantry Division is on its way to join a convoy to offer it protection. Due to the often dense vegetation found in South Vietnam, many of the combat encounters in which the vehicle found itself were done at almost point-blank range. The enemy favoured these engagements as it often proved impossible for American soldiers on the ground to call in artillery or air support for fear of killing their own men. (*National Archives*)

(*Opposite page*) The M134 7.62mm minigun seen here on an M113 series APC was originally designed for use on US Army and US Air Force helicopters during the Vietnam War. The M134 7.62mm mini-gun was also mounted on the US Air Force C-47 Spooky gunships as they could not support the weight of the heavier 20mm M61 six-barrelled cannons. (*National Archives*)

(*Above*) The crew of this US Marine Corps LVTP-5A1 in South Vietnam has added a parapet of sandbags for added protection, upon which they have mounted a 7.62mm M60 machine-gun. The driver's position was on the front left-hand side of the hull, with the vehicle commander being located on the front right-hand side of the hull. The passengers are huddled on the roof of the vehicle for safety from mines once ashore. (*Marine Corps Historical Center*)

(*Opposite above*) The US Army saw a need for a mechanized infantry combat vehicle as early as 1963. As it would be several years before such a vehicle would be available to test, it was decided to modify a small number of M113 series APCs with gun ports as an interim fighting vehicle. When modified, the vehicle was designated the XM734 and some were sent to Southeast Asia for troop evaluations. They were not considered successful. (*Patton Museum*)

(*Opposite below*) Exiting the ocean is a US Marine Corps LVTP-5A1. The large steel-armoured hull of the vehicle had an inverted V-shaped bow and bottom to improve its water handling characteristics. There was a large hydraulically operated ramp at the front of the vehicle's hull with the engine located in the rear of the hull. (*Marine Corps Historical Center*)

A platoon of US Marine Corps LVTP-5A1s is shown on patrol in South Vietnam. The box-like superstructure on the rear of the vehicle's roof housed the engine air intake and exhaust system. The previous model of the vehicle lacked this superstructure. There were escape hatches on either side of the vehicle's hull. (*Marine Corps Historical Center*)

Besides the US Army, there were other users of the M113 series APC during the Vietnam War. These included the Australian Army M113A1 APCs seen here. The three vehicles in the foreground have been fitted with the American-designed and built turrets armed with twin .30 calibre machine-guns. (*Patton Museum*)

Two Australian Army M113A1s APCs are seen on patrol in South Vietnam. As a point of interest, both vehicles have their machine-gun-armed turrets traversed to the rear. It seems the commanders on both vehicles prefer using the .30 calibre machine-guns mounted on the top of the turrets as their weapon of choice. (*Patton Museum*)

To reinforce what is seen in the previous photograph. This overhead photograph of an Australian Army M113A1 on patrol in South Vietnam shows that the vehicle commander has mounted a 7.62mm M60 machine-gun on the roof of his machine-gun-armed turret. It appears that the twin barrels on the machine-gun turrets have their dust covers fitted. (*Patton Museum*)

(*Above*) On display at the Israeli Tank Museum, officially known as The Armoured Corps Memorial Site and Museum, located at Latrun, Israel, is an example of the Soviet-designed and built BTR-40 APC. The vehicle was 18 feet (5.5m) in length and had a height of 6 feet (1.8m). Vehicle width was 6.25 feet (1.9m). (*Vladimir Yakubov*)

(*Opposite above*) Forming part of the collection of the Virginia Museum of Military Vehicles is a Soviet-designed and built BTR-152. This particular example is a command vehicle as it features an armoured roof, a feature not seen on the standard APC version. The vehicle was 22 feet (6.8m) in length and the APC version had a height of 6.5 feet (2.0m). Vehicle width was 7 feet (2.3m). (*Michael Green*)

(*Opposite below*) Shown on the famous Ho Chin Minh Trail is an NVA BTR-40. The trail/road system ran from North Vietnam through Laos and Cambodia into South Vietnam and was the pathway for the supplies and personnel that kept the war in South Vietnam going throughout the Vietnam War. Despite endless efforts by the American military to sever the Ho Chi Minh trail system by aerial assault, it was never successful. (*Patton Museum*)

(*Above*) On display at the US Marine Corps base Camp Pendleton in Southern California is this Chinese-developed and built Type-63 APC. Widely exported and employed by the NVA during the Vietnam War, this particular vehicle was captured by the Marine Corps from the Iraqi Army during Operation Iraqi Freedom in 2003. (*Paul Hannah*)

(*Opposite above*) In the possession of the US Army back in the early 1980s as an Opposing Forces (OPFOR) training vehicle is this Soviet-developed and built BTR-60PB APC. The vehicle was 25 feet (7.6m) long and 7 feet (2.3m) in height. Vehicle width was 7 feet (2.3m). Combat use by the Soviet Army in Afghanistan showed that the vehicle was extremely vulnerable to heavy machine-gunfire. (*Michael Green*)

(*Opposite below*) Among the many Soviet-developed and built vehicles on display at the Israeli Tank Museum is this amphibious BTR-50PK APC. The vehicle had a length of 22 feet (6.7m) and a height of 6 feet (1.8m). The width of the vehicle was 10.5 feet (3.2m.) Due to the cramped nature of the vehicle's troop compartment and lack of firing ports, the passengers had to dismount to fight. (*Vladimir Yakubov*)

Chapter Three

Armoured Fighting Vehicles

The First Indochina War and follow-on Vietnam War saw the use of a wide variety of miscellaneous armoured fighting vehicles (AFVs). In some cases these vehicles were variants of existing tanks and armoured personnel carriers but normally built in smaller numbers. Variants are popular with armies as they typically shorten the research and development period for any new vehicle. It also eases an army's logistical burden as the bulk of a vehicle's parts are in the supply system and simplifies the training time for maintenance personnel who are already familiar with the basic vehicle chassis.

To make up for its shortages of armoured fighting vehicles in Indochina, the CEFEO took into service the French-designed and built armoured car, referred to as the Panhard et Levassor Type 178B. Production of the Type 178B began in 1945 for the new French Army. It was armed with a 47mm main gun and a 7.5mm coaxial machine-gun. The original version of the vehicle weighed 18,078lb (8.2mt) and was powered by a gasoline engine that gave it a top speed of 45mph (72km/h) and an approximate operational range of 186 miles (300km). The front of the Type 178B was protected by 25mm of armour.

British AFVs with the CEFEO

The CEFEO also used the universal carrier, left over from British Army Commonwealth occupation of southern Indochina. This small, open-topped vehicle originally entered British Army service in 1940. It weighed 8,848lb (4mt) and was powered by a gasoline engine that gave it a top speed on level roads of 32mph (51km/h) and an approximate operational range of 160 miles (256km) on level roads. With a crew of four or five, the vehicle was protected on its front by armour 12mm thick. In CEFEO service, it was armed with an assortment of machine-guns and used as a reconnaissance vehicle.

In addition to the universal carrier, the CEFEO acquired two different types of British-designed and built armoured cars: the Coventry Mk I armoured car and the Humber scout car Mk I/II. Both were of Second World War vintage. The Coventry Mk I armoured car weighed 22,818lb (10.35mt) and was powered by a gasoline engine that gave it a top speed of 42mph (68km/h) and an approximate operational range of 250 miles (400km.) The four-man vehicle was armed with a turret-mounted 2-pounder (40mm) main gun and a single coaxial 7.92mm Besa machine-gun. Maximum armour protection on the front of the vehicle was 14mm.

The turret-less Humber Scout Car Mk I/II weighed 5,512lb (2.5mt) and was powered by a gasoline engine that provided it with a top speed of 62mph (100km/h) and an approximate operational range of 200 miles (320km). The Mk II version of the Humber scout car had a different transmission from the original Mk I model. The two-man vehicle in British Army service was armed only with one or two Bren 7.7mm machine-guns. Maximum armour protection on the front of the Humber Scout Car Mk I/II was 14mm. Pictorial evidence indicates that some of them in service with the CEFEO had improvised, open-topped machine-gun-equipped turrets fitted.

American AFVs with the CEFEO

Brought to Indochina by the CEFEO were wheeled armoured fighting vehicles that the Free French Army had acquired from the American Government during and after the Second World War. These included the M3A1 scout car and the light-armoured car M8. The M3A1 first entered US Army service in 1940 and the M8 in 1943. Both the M3A1 and the M8 were open-topped and intended primarily for reconnaissance duties.

The M3A1 had a crew of six to eight men and was typically armed with a single .50 calibre machine-gun and two .30 calibre machine-guns mounted on a skate rail. The four-man M8 had a turret-mounted 37mm main gun and a roof-mounted .50 calibre machine-gun. The M3A1 weighed 12,400lb (5.62mt) and the M8 17,400lb (7.9mt). Both were powered by gasoline engines. The M3A1 had a top speed of 50mph (80km/h) on level roads and the M8 a top speed of 55mph (89km/h.) Armour protection on the front of the M3A1 topped out at 13mm and that on the M8 at 16mm.

Employed by the CEFEO in Indochina was the US-built four-man howitzer motor carriage M8 armed with a short-barrel 75mm howitzer, based on the chassis of the M5 light tank, the predecessor to the M5A1 light tank that also saw service with the CEFEO. The vehicle was accepted into service by the US Army in 1942 and had also been supplied to the Free French Army during the Second World War under Lend-Lease. The vehicle weighed 34,600lb (16mt) and was powered by a gasoline engine that gave it a top speed of 36mph (58km/h) and an approximate operational range on level roads of 100 miles (161km). The maximum armour protection on the front of the M8 was 25mm.

A Second World War amphibious tractor configured as an assault gun that saw service with the CEFEO in Indochina was the LVT(A)5. The suffix 'A' in the vehicle's designation stood for armoured. The LVT(A)5 was based on the chassis of the

LVT(A)1 but was fitted with a new, open-topped turret (borrowed from the howitzer motor carriage M8) armed with a 75mm howitzer and originally a .50 calibre machine-gun, later replaced by two .30 calibre machine-guns. The LVT(A)5 could be used in the direct fire or indirect-fire mode.

The six-man LVT(A)5 weighed approximately 40,000lb (18mt) and was powered by a gasoline engine that provided a top speed on land of 25mph (40km/h) and 7mph (11km/h) in water. The vehicle had an approximate operational range of 125 miles (201km) on land and 75 miles (121km) in the water. The maximum armour thickness on the front of the LVT(A)5 was 51mm.

Fearing the possibility that Red Chinese Army armoured units might come to the assistance of the Viet Minh, the CEFEO deployed to northern Indochina the American-designed and built 90mm gun motor carriage (GMC) M36B2. Besides its 90mm main gun, the M36B2 was often fitted on its roof with a .50 calibre machine-gun. The five-man vehicle weighed 63,000lb (29mt) and had a top speed of 26mph (42km/h) and an approximate operational range on level roads of 150 miles (241km).

US Army AFVs in Vietnam

A variant of the M41 series light tank employed by the US Army and the ARVN during the Vietnam War was the twin 40mm-self-propelled antiaircraft gun M42 and M42A1. The vehicle was also known by its nick-name as the Duster. Originally intended as an antiaircraft vehicle, the six-man M42A1 saw widespread use during the Vietnam War in a ground support role, guarding artillery bases from enemy infantry assaults and as convoy escorts. Powered by a gasoline engine, the M42A1 had a top speed on roads of 45mph (72km/h) and an approximate operational range of 120 miles (193km). The maximum armour protection on the front of the open-topped vehicle was 25mm.

A variant of the M48A3 medium tank employed during the Vietnam War by the US Marine Corps with great success was armed with a flame gun in lieu of the standard 90mm main gun, and designated the M67A2 flame thrower tank. Stored within the vehicle was the main fuel container with a total capacity of 398 gallons. This provided the M67A2 flame thrower tank with approximately one minute of firing duration. The three-man crews that served upon them nicknamed them flames or Zippos, after the well-known cigarette lighter.

A vehicle deployed to South Vietnam by the US Army, which one might assume was armoured but in fact was not, had the official designator of 90mm, full-tracked, self-propelled gun M56. Another title for the vehicle was the SPAT (self-propelled antitank). It was also referred to by the nick-name Scorpion. Built out of aluminium alloy and weighing only 15,500lb (7mt) the small, lightweight, four-man vehicle was intended to be either parachuted into a landing zone seized by American airborne troops/air assault troops or landed by glider or transport aircraft. Powered by a gasoline engine, the M56 had a top speed on roads of 28mph (45km/h) and an approximate operational range of 140 miles (225km) on roads. It remained in South Vietnam until replaced by the M551 Sheridan beginning in early 1969.

Convoy escort vehicles

As the majority of the far-flung bases operated by the American military in South Vietnam required re-supply by truck convoys, there was a pressing need to protect vulnerable, unarmoured logistic vehicles from ambushes by the VC or NVA. As this was somewhat of an un-planned role for the US Army and the US Marine Corps, there were no vehicles then in service that were optimized for this role. While the M48A3 tank and the M113 APC often performed this job to great success, there were never enough of them available and they were much more useful in offensive operations aimed at destroying the enemy in their lairs.

With the lack of suitable vehicles for protecting convoys, American military truckers quickly decided to take matters into their own hands. They began arming and armouring some of their trucks to turn them into makeshift armoured fighting vehicles, popularly referred to as gun trucks. Without a template, the resulting un-authorized machine-gun-armed gun trucks came in a wide array of shapes and sizes, based on whatever material, imagination and weapons were at hand. The typical platform for the greatest majority of gun trucks was the standard US Army/US Marine Corps M54 5-ton cargo truck (the 5-ton refers to the cross-country carrying capacity of the vehicle and not the weight of the vehicle), or the smaller M35 2½-ton cargo truck.

The US Army realized early on the need by the ARVN for a suitable wheeled convoy protection vehicle to replace their aging fleet of M8 light armoured cars inherited from the CEFEO. The US Army turned to American private industry for an answer. What soon caught their interest was a vehicle designed by the Cadillac Gage Company in 1962. It was a machine-gun-armed armoured car that they originally referred to as the Commando and later as the V-100. After a number of suggested modifications the vehicle was placed into production for the ARVN in 1964 as the XM706 and the first units shipped to South Vietnam in 1965.

ARVN success with the XM706 attracted the interest of US Army Military Police units in South Vietnam who had been recently tasked with guarding truck supply convoys. They got their own slightly modified XM706s in 1968 that were designated the XM706E1.

There were never enough of the XM706E1s to protect all of the US Army truck convoys running in South Vietnam. However, they did prove a welcome supplement to the improvised gun trucks. Eventually the XM706E1 was accepted into US Army service as the M706. There was also an open-topped version of the vehicle, designated the XM706E2, intended for used by US Air Force personnel to guard air bases in South Vietnam, which proved popular targets for the VC and NVA.

The M706 weighed 16,250lb (7mt) and was powered by a gasoline engine that provided it a top speed of 61.5mph (99km/h) and a maximum operational range on level roads of 600 miles (965km). With a crew of up to eleven men, the vehicle's authorized armament included different types of 7.62mm turret-mounted machine-guns. In South Vietnam it was not uncommon for additional machine-guns, including a .50 calibre machine-gun to be added to the vehicle to boost its firepower. The maximum armour protection on the front of the M706 was 9.5mm.

US Army M113 variants

Besides the standard M113/M113A1 APC employed during the Vietnam War as an ACAV, other versions of the vehicle also took part in the conflict. This reflected the original US Army requirements that it serve as a platform for a wide variety of different roles. Those that served in South Vietnam that retained the same general appearance of the standard APC version included a mortar carrier version armed with either an 81mm or 107mm (4.2 inch) mortar in the rear hull compartment.

When based on the gasoline-engine-powered M113, the 107mm mortar-equipped version was designated the M106. Mounted on the diesel-engine-powered M113A1, the 81mm mortar-armed version became the M125A1 and the 107mm mortar-equipped version became the M106A1. The US Army and the ARVN employed both the M125A1 and the M106A1. The Australian Army employed the M125A1 during their time in South Vietnam.

This passage from a 1967 US Army report entitled *Mechanized and Combat Operations in Vietnam* describes a problem with the M106A1 armed with a 107mm mortar during combat engagements:

> Tanks and mechanized infantry battalions are constantly confronted with two basic problems in employing their organic 4.2 inch [107mm] mortar platoons: the nature of the war in RVN [Republic of Vietnam] requires the capability to quickly deliver fires in any direction; and the minimum range of the 4.2 inch mortar (840 meters) [919 yards] normally precludes their use in firing missions directly in front of the perimeter in which they are positioned.

There was a Model B gun shield kit for the mortar-carrier versions of the M113 that included only the open-topped circular armour turret tub for the vehicle commander's .50 calibre machine-gun and not the two offset shield-protected M60 machine-guns. Pictorial evidence shows that some of the crews of the mortar-equipped M113s used the Model A gun shield gun.

The US Army began studying the possibility of mounting flamethrower kits on tanks during the Second World War. Post-war, the US Army was considering using the M59 APC as a platform for their newly developed flamethrower kit. However, as the gasoline-engine powered M113 APC was beginning to enter service in 1960 they switched the design work to the new vehicle. The end result was the introduction of the M132 in 1963 armed with the flamethrower M108 mounted in a cupola armed with a coaxial 7.62mm machine-gun.

It was soon decided to mount the flamethrower M108 in the new diesel engine powered M113A1 resulting in the M132A1. Both models of the vehicles served during the Vietnam War. Additional fuel for the flamethrowers on the M132 and M132A1 was transported in an armoured version of the M548 cargo carrier designated as the XM45E1. The M548 cargo carrier was itself merely a non-armoured version of the M113/M113A1.

The use of the flamethrower versions of the M113 during the Vietnam War appears in this extract from a US Army report entitled *Mechanized and Combat Operations in Vietnam* that is dated March 1967:

> The M132 mechanized flamethrower has been successfully employed in offensive and defensive operations in RVN [Republic of Vietnam]. In search and destroy operations, they are normally employed in pairs against bunkers and densely foliaged enemy-defended areas containing antipersonnel mines and booby traps. Flame directed at such areas may not destroy a protected enemy, but heat detonates mines and defoliates the area. In defensive positions, the flamethrower is employed to fill gaps not covered by direct fire weapons and to illuminate the area. During movements, the M132s can provide close-in flank protection to the column.

Six units of an antiaircraft version of the M113 family of vehicles were deployed to South Vietnam in 1968 as a test. They were armed with a six-barrel 20mm Gatling-type gun mounted in a power-operated turret. The weapon was optically guided with a range-only radar for engaging aerial targets. The weapon system was mounted on a modified diesel-engine-powered M113A1, designated the XM741. The prefix 'X' meant experimental. Mated together, the weapon and vehicle eventually became the M163A1 Vulcan Air Defense System and saw use in the Vietnam War as a convoy escort vehicle.

US Army self-propelled artillery in Vietnam

Deployed to South Vietnam by the US Army were the 155mm self-propelled howitzer M109 and its near identical counterpart, the 105mm self-propelled howitzer M108. The six-man M109 weighed 54,461lb (25mt) and the smaller five-man M108 weighed 46,221lb (21mt). Both were powered by diesel engines that gave them a top speed on level roads of 35mph (56km/h) and an approximate operational range of 220 miles (354km).

Besides their howitzers, both the M109 and M108 were armed with a roof-mounted .50 calibre machine-gun for self-protection. Unlike the steel clad M53, both the M109 and the M108 were built out of aluminium alloy armour that had a maximum thickness on the front of the vehicles of 32mm. Production of these two vehicles had begun in 1963.

There were two additional self-propelled artillery pieces deployed to South Vietnam by the US Army, the 175mm self-propelled gun M107 and the 8-inch howitzer M110. Both went into production between 1961 and 1962 and were mounted on the same lightweight chassis suitable for air transportation. The only armour on the vehicles was 13mm of steel armour around the driver's compartment.

The M107 weighed 62,100lb (28mt) and the M110 58,500lb (27mt). Both were powered by diesel engines that gave them a top speed on land of 34mph (55km/h) and an approximate operational range of 450 miles (724km) on level roads. There was seating for five men on both vehicles with the remainder of the crew riding on a non-armoured M113-based ammunition resupply vehicle designated the M548.

Marine Corps AFVs in Vietnam

The US Marine Corps deployed to South Vietnam an extremely small, ungainly looking vehicle officially named the Ontos. It was first conceived in 1951 as a light-weight armoured tracked vehicle that could be modified to serve a variety of roles, including as an antitank vehicle armed with varying numbers of recoilless rifles. The antitank version of the vehicle was accepted for service in 1955 as the multiple 106mm self-propelled rifle M50, with the US Marine Corps ordering 297 units. It was armed with six 106mm recoilless rifles, three on either side of the M50 hull, which had to be reloaded from outside the vehicle. There was also a .30 calibre machine-gun mounted on the vehicle. A .50 calibre spotting rifle was only used to support engagements by the 106mm main weapons.

The three-man M50 weighed 16,200lb (7.34mt) and was powered by a gasoline engine that gave a top speed of 30mph (48km/h) on roads and a maximum opera-tional range of approximately 150 miles (241km) on level roads. An improved version with a more powerful gasoline engine was designated the M50A1 and was the model deployed to South Vietnam. Armour protection on the vehicle topped out at 13mm. The vehicle proved very susceptible to the entire range of enemy antitank weapons.

A variant of the LVTP5(A)1 employed during the Vietnam War by the US Marine Corps was the LVTH6. It was armed with a turret-mounted 105mm howitzer, a coaxial .30 calibre machine-gun, a turret-mounted .50 calibre machine-gun and was actually the first vehicle built of what would become the LVTP5 family of vehicles. The LVTH6 had a seven-man crew consisting of the vehicle commander, driver, crew chief, gunner, loader and two ammunition handlers. The vehicle's 105mm howitzer could be employed in either the direct fire or indirect fire mode.

The LVTH6 would occasionally see productive use during the Vietnam War, which is recounted in this passage from author Kenneth W. Estes' book entitled *Marines under Armor: The Marine Corps and the Armored Fighting Vehicle, 1916–2000*:

On 10 December [1967] the attached infantry spotted a reinforced platoon of NVA and pursued. The battalion commander, Lt. Col. Edward R. Toner, called in two provisional rifle platoons from his B Company, accompanied by two LVTH6s as assault guns. The following day, these moved in on the NVA. The H6s fired at 50–150 meters [55–164 yards] and the other four H6s provided indirect fire support. The NVA counterattacked but died in battle, leaving 54 dead and uncovered a supply dump and mortar position. The cost to friendlies was only 20 wounded.

Marine Corps self-propelled artillery

A couple of self-propelled artillery pieces employed during the early years of the Vietnam War by the US Marine Corps were the 155mm self-propelled gun M53 and its near identical cousin, the 8-inch self-propelled howitzer M55. Production of these vehicles began in 1952. Both vehicles incorporated components from the M46, M47 and M48 Patton tank series of medium tanks.

The six-man M53 weighed 100,000lb (45mt) and the six-man M55 98,000lb (44mt). Both were powered by a gasoline engine that provided them a top speed on level roads of 35mph (56km/h). The vehicles had an approximate operational range of 150 miles (241km) on level roads. Besides their main guns, the vehicle crews had a roof-mounted .50 calibre machine-gun for self-protection. The maximum armour thickness on the front of the M53 and the M55 was 25mm. The M53 and M55 were eventually replaced in US Marine Corps service in South Vietnam by the 155mm self-propelled howitzer M109.

Australian AFV

The Australian Army deployed a very interesting home-grown vehicle to South Vietnam referred to as the M113A1 Fire Support Vehicle (FSV.) It consisted of a standard M113A1 APC modified to mount a 76mm main gun armed-turret from the British-designed and built post-Second World War armoured car named the Saladin. The requirement for the vehicle originated in 1966 as a stop-gap prior to the Australian Army possibly acquiring the American-designed and built M551.

The FSV entered into Australian Army service between 1970 and 1971 with the first four arriving in South Vietnam in the late summer of 1971. The three-man vehicle weighed 26,266lb (11.9mt) and was powered by a diesel engine that gave it a top speed of 42mph (68km/h) and a maximum operational range on level roads of 300 miles (483km). Besides the 76mm main gun, secondary armament on the FSV consisted of two .30 calibre machine-guns, one being the coaxial. The maximum armour thickness on the front of the vehicle was 32mm.

Army of the Republic of South Vietnam AFV

The US Government began supplying the ARVN with the amphibious M114 armoured command and reconnaissance vehicle in 1963. There was also another model known as the M114A1. The difference between the two models revolved around the roof-mounted .50 calibre machine-gun operated by the vehicle commander. On the M114, he had to fire the weapon manually with his head and upper torso exposed above his cupola. On the M114A1, the vehicle commander could fire the .50 calibre machine-gun remotely from within the relative safety of his vehicle.

The M114/M114A1 had a crew of three men and a seat for a fourth. Some of those employed by the US Army were eventually fitted with a remote-controlled 20mm gun-armed cupola in place of the cupola mounting the .50 calibre machine-gun, with a designator of M114E1 during the testing phase. When standardized they were known as the M114A2.

Weighing in at 15,093lb (6.8mt) in the case of the M114 and 15,276lb (7mt) with the M114A1, the three-man vehicle was powered by a gasoline engine that gave it a top speed of 36mph (58km/h) on land and 3.6mph (5.8km/h) in water. The maximum operational range of the M114 on level roads was 275 miles (443km). Maximum armour protection on the front of the aluminium alloy vehicle was 44mm.

Once in service with the ARVN, the M114 turned out to be a major disappointment as the vehicle did not have the same off-road mobility as the M113. Compounding the problem was the fact that the M114 was far less resistant to mine damage than the M113 and less reliable. This resulted in the US Army advisors to the ARVN having the vehicle pulled from service by 1964 and replaced with the far more useful M113.

North Vietnamese Army AFVs

From the war reserve stocks of the Soviet Army, the NVA was reported by one reference source as having received the entire range of Second World War-era Red Army self-propelled guns, ranging from the small SU-76 all the way up to the massive ISU-152. Except for a single photograph of an SU-100 in NVA service, there is no pictorial evidence that these vehicles were employed during the Vietnam War by the

NVA. The ARVN, US units and Allies never reported encountering any of these vehicles in combat.

Based on the chassis of the T-70 light tank the turret-less and open-topped SU-76 had a crew of four men and was armed with 76.2mm gun in a fixed casemate with limited traverse and elevation. It served with the Red Army from 1943 until the end of the Second World War. Maximum armour protection on the front of the vehicle was 35mm.

The four-man SU-100 was based on the chassis of the T-34 medium tank, with its 100mm main gun mounted in an armoured casemate on the front hull of the vehicle, with limited traverse and elevation. The vehicle weighed 69,665lb (32mt) and production for the Red Army began in September 1944. Powered by a diesel engine, the vehicle had a top speed of 30mph (48km/h) and an approximate operational range on level roads of 200 miles (320km). Armour protection on the front of the vehicle was 45mm. There was no secondary armament carried on the vehicle.

The NVA received from the Soviet Union two different full-tracked anti-aircraft vehicles; the older of the vehicles was designated the ZSU-57-2 and the newer one referred to as the ZSU-23-4. The six-man ZSU-57-2 first entered service with the Soviet Army in 1957 with the chassis based on components of the T-54 medium tank.

The heart of the ZSU-57-2 was its large, open-topped turret that contained two 57mm antiaircraft guns each capable of firing 120 rounds per minute. However, typically storage on the vehicle was for only 316 rounds. There was no radar system on the ZSU-57-2, only optical sights that restricted its use to daylight fair weather conditions. The vehicle weighed 61,949lb (28.1mt) and was powered by a diesel engine that gave it a top speed of 30mph (48km/h) and an approximate operational range of 248 miles (400km). The maximum armour protection on the front of the ZSU-57-2 was 15mm.

The ZSU-57-2 was replaced in Soviet Army service starting in the early 1960s by the 30,864lb (14mt) ZSU-23-4. The four-man vehicle was based on the GM-575 tracked vehicle chassis and some components from the PT-76 amphibious tank. Only limited numbers of the ZSU-23-4 saw action with NVA units, and only during the last stages of the Vietnam War.

The killing power of the ZSU-23-4 is based upon an arrangement of four, water-cooled 23mm automatic cannons each capable of firing 800–1,000 rounds per minute. As the vehicle only carries 2,000 stowed rounds, the cannons are typically fired in short bursts of no more than 50 rounds. Unlike, the ZSU-57-2, the ZSU-23-4 is radar guided with a backup optical fire-control system and can be fired on the move. The vehicle weighs 30,864lb (14mt) and is powered by a diesel engine that provided it with a top speed of 27mph (44km/h) and an approximate operational range of 161 miles (260km). The maximum armour protection on the front of the ZSU-23-4 was 15mm.

(*Above*) Seen here in service with the CEFEO in Indochina is a British-designed and built Coventry Mk I armoured car. There were 283 (63 in 1944 and 220 in 1945) units of the Second World War vintage armoured car built. It was 15 feet 5 inches (4.72m) in length and had a width of 8 feet 8 inches (2.68m). The vehicle had a height of 7 feet 9 inches (2.35m). (*Tank Museum*)

(*Opposite above*) Members of the Vietnamese National Army are shown standing next to their French-designed and built Type 178B armoured car. Instead of the original turret armed with a 25mm main gun, this version of the vehicle was armed with a 47mm main gun in a new, much larger turret. The armoured car had an assistant driver in the rear hull that allowed it be driven in either direction without turning the vehicle. (*Patton Museum*)

(*Opposite below*) On display at an open day held once a year by the Virginia Museum of Military Vehicles is a British-designed and built Universal Carrier. The vehicle is 12 feet 4 inches (3.75m) in length and has a width of 6 feet 11 inches (2.10m). Vehicle height was 5 feet 3 inches (1.60m). It could cross a 5 foot 3 inch (1.62m) wide trench and climb a 60 degree gradient. (*Michael Green*)

(*Above*) Belonging to the Belgian National Military Museum is this British-designed and built Humber scout car. A total of 4,102 units of the vehicle were constructed in various versions as a backup design to the better known Daimler Dingo. The vehicle was 12 feet 7 inches (3.87m) in length and 6 feet 2 inches (1.89m) wide. Vehicle height was 7 feet (2.13m). (*Pierre Olivier-BUAN*)

(*Opposite above*) Belonging to the Military Vehicle Technology Foundation is this restored M3A1 scout car. A total of 20,984 units of the vehicle were built between 1940 and 1944, with over half being exported under Lend-Lease. The CEFEO must have acquired the M3A1s they brought to Indochina from the huge vehicle stockpiles left over at the conclusion of the Second World War. (*Michael Green*)

(*Opposite below*) An M3A1 scout car serving with the CEFEO in Indochina is covered with foliage. One could think it was for camouflage. More likely it was being used as cover from the sun, as the normal canvas cover fitted over the troop compartment seems to be missing from this vehicle. (*Patton Museum*)

(*Above*) A useful addition to the inventory of the Free French Army during the Second World War was the American-designed and built 75mm howitzer motor carriage M8, based on the modified chassis of the M5 light tank. The driver and assistant driver lacked overhead hatches on the M8 and entered and left the vehicle via the open-topped turret. (*Patton Museum*)

(*Opposite above*) Seen on patrol in Indochina is a CEFEO M8 light armoured car. American factories assembled 8,523 units of the vehicle between March 1943 and May 1945. The US Army was never happy with the vehicle's poor off-road performance and desired a full-tracked reconnaissance vehicle. (*Patton Museum*)

(*Opposite below*) Pictured in Europe is this restored M8 light armoured car in US Army Second World War markings. The vehicle is 16 feet 5 inches (5.03m) in length and 8 feet 4 inches (2.59m) wide. The height of the vehicle is 7 feet 4.5 inches (2.26m). It could climb a vertical wall 12 inches (30.1cm) high and ford a water obstacle of 24 inches (61cm). (*Pierre Olivier-BUAN*)

(*Above*) On display in France as a monument vehicle is this 75mm howitzer motor carriage M8. The vehicle had authorized storage space for forty-six main gun rounds and mounted either the 75mm howitzer M2 or M3. It had a length of 16 feet 4 inches (5m) and a width of 7 feet 7.5 inches (2.35m). It was 7 feet 7 inches (2.35m) in height. (*Pierre-Olivier BUAN*)

(*Opposite above*) Belonging to the Tank Museum located at Saumur, France, is this American-designed and built LVTA4 or LVTA5 amphibious tractor, which has been restored to running condition. The LVTA4 was first introduced into American military service in March 1944 and armed with a 75mm howitzer. (*Christopher Vallier*)

(*Opposite below*) Pictured are three LVTA4 or LVTA5 amphibious tractors in service with the CEFEO in Indochina. The vehicle in the foreground features an improvised sun shield. The 75mm howitzer on the LVTA4/5 was approximately 4 feet 6 inches long (1.4m) and had a top rate of fire of eight rounds per minute. The maximum range of the weapon was 9,650 yards (8,824m.) Patton Museum)

(Above) Shown in American military markings is this LVTA4 amphibious tractor. This vehicle and the slightly upgraded LVTA5 were 26 feet 1 inch (8m) in length and had a width of 10 feet 8 inches (3.29m). The height of the vehicles was 10 feet 2.5 inches (3.11m). There was room in the vehicles to store 100 of the 75mm main gun rounds. *(FMC)*

(Right) In the service of the CEFEO in Indochina is this American-designed and built M36B2 tank destroyer. It is a late production vehicle, as is evident by the folding armoured turret top and the muzzle brake. The vehicle's crew added an improvised .50 calibre machine-gun mount on the front portion of the vehicle's turret. *(Patton Museum)*

The M36B tank destroyer pictured has the late production muzzle brake on its 90mm main gun, but lacks the other features seen on the examples employed by the CEFEO in Indochina. The vehicle was 24 feet 6 inches (7.5m) in length and had a width of 10 feet (3.05m). With a machine-gun fitted on the rear roof the vehicle was 10 feet 9 inches (3.32m) tall. *(TACOM)*

Minus its flash hiders, this US Army twin 40mm self-propelled gun M42A1 stands watch at an American military base in South Vietnam. The vehicle had storage space for 480 rounds of 40mm ammunition that was fired from four round clips. In the power operated mode, the twin 40mm cannons could be elevated 25 degrees a second and traversed 360 degrees in nine seconds. *(National Archives)*

(*Above*) The crew of a US Army twin 40mm self-propelled gun M42A1 are shown engaging the enemy during a convoy protection mission in South Vietnam. Each cannon could be fired at 120 rounds per minute for a combined total of 240 rounds per minute. (*National Archives*)

(*Opposite above*) Dominating the South Vietnamese terrain around it is this US Army twin 40mm self-propelled gun M42A1. The large door located on the front hull of the vehicle, in between the driver's position on the left side and the vehicle commander position on the right, was employed to pass ammunition into the vehicle when reloading. (*National Archives*)

(*Opposite below*) Shown in use during the Vietnam War is this US Marine Corps M67A2 flamethrower tank, which was based on a modified M48A3 tank chassis. Notice that the vehicle commander has dispensed with the cupola-mounted .50 calibre machine-gun and in its place has mounted a .30 calibre machine-gun on the cupola roof. (*Patton Museum*)

(*Above*) The impressive sheet of fire coming out of the flame gun on a US Marine Corps M67A2 flame thrower tank in South Vietnam was to burn off the local vegetation to deny the enemy concealment. The Marine Corps had seventy-three of its older generation M67A1 flame thrower tanks, based on the M48A2 medium tank, converted to the M48A3 medium tank configuration. (*Marine Corps Historical Center*)

(*Opposite above*) This side view of a US Marine Corps M67A2 flamethrower tank shows the slightly shorter and thicker fake barrel that helps to identify the vehicle, as compared to the standard M48A3 medium tank armed with a 90mm main gun. There is even a phoney muzzle brake and bore evacuator mounted on the fake barrel of the M67A2. (*TACOM*)

(*Opposite below*) A military vehicle completely unsuited for employment during the Vietnam War was the 90mm full-tracked self-propelled gun M56, better known to most by its Scorpion nickname. The unarmoured vehicle was armed with a 90mm main gun whose recoil would lift the entire front of the vehicle off the ground when fired. (*TACOM*)

(*Above*) The 90mm full-tracked self-propelled gun M56 is seen here being employed during the Vietnam War. Visible in this photograph is the twenty-nine-round ammunition rack located just below the breech of the vehicle's main gun. Also seen in use is the fold-down platform on the rear of the vehicle to provide working space for the loader. (*TACOM*)

(*Opposite above*) A trio of US Army M35 2½ ton series cargo trucks have been armoured in a similar fashion. The vehicles pictured seem to be configured as armoured troop carriers rather than what was generally referred to as gun trucks during the Vietnam War. Visible are some M60 7.62mm machine-guns, but not the typical .50 calibre machine-guns seen on most gun trucks during the conflict. (*National Archives*)

(*Opposite below*) Pictured is a recreation of a Vietnam War-era M54 5-ton series gun truck being demonstrated during a gathering of military vehicle collectors in England. The Vietnamese writing on the side of the truck is to warn civilians and their vehicles from getting too close to the sides. (*Christophe Vallier*)

A recreation of a Vietnam War era M54 5-ton series gun truck armed with the M55 quad machine-gun turret during a military vehicle collector's rally in England. The machine-gun mount was designed and built by the American W.L. Maxson Corporation during the Second World War and is commonly referred to as the Maxson mount. *(Christophe Vallier)*

In some cases US Army truckers in the Vietnam War dispensed with improvised armour arrangements on their vehicle and strapped a damaged M113 APC, minus its suspension system, as is seen here. Besides the standard .50 calibre machine-gun in the vehicle's commander cupola, there are two more on the roof of the rear passenger compartment. *(Patton Museum)*

Pictured is the pilot Cadillac Gage Commando armoured car being tested by the US Army in 1963 for consideration for use in South Vietnam by the ARVN. The vehicle was later designated as the V-100. Testing of the pilot vehicles in the United States and South Vietnam led to some design changes that resulted in a production vehicle for the ARVN designated the XM706. *(Patton Museum)*

US Army Military Police interest in the ARVN's successful employment of the XM706 armoured car led to the adoption of a slightly modified version by the US Army in 1968, an example of which is shown here. It was originally designated the XM706E1, later standardized as the M706. In lieu of the original M113 APC periscopes, the M706 had laminated vision blocks. *(Jim Mesko collection)*

(*Above*) Escorting a convoy in South Vietnam is a US Army Military Police M706. The US Army Military Police originally requested that the M706 one-man manually-operated turret be armed with a .50 calibre machine-gun and a coaxial .30 calibre machine-gun. Due to a shortage of .50 calibre machine-guns at the time of production, the vehicle went into service with two .30 calibre turret-mounted machine-guns. (*Jim Mesko collection*)

(*Opposite above*) Two US Army Military Police M706s stand guard in South Vietnam. The rear hull-mounted gasoline engine in the vehicle was the same as found in the M113 APC. The large tires on the M706 were specially developed by Cadillac Gage and contained metal liners that allowed them to operate for at least 50 miles after being punctured. (*Jim Mesko collection*)

(*Opposite below*) On display at Fort Leonard Wood, Missouri, is a US Army M706. The vehicle was 18 feet 8 inches (5.69m) in length and 7 feet 5 inches (2.26m) in width. To the top of its dual machine-gun-armed turret the M706 was 8 feet (2.45m) in height. There was authorized storage on the vehicle for 8,580 rounds of 7.62mm ammunition. (*Paul Hannah*)

Forming part of the Ropkey Armour Museum in Indiana is a restored, Second World War vintage, US Army M8 light armoured car in the foreground and behind it a Vietnam War-era M706. The M706 survived in American Government service until the mid-1980s guarding various nuclear sites around the country, with a few later passing into police service as SWAT team vehicles. *(Michael Green)*

Initially, US Air Force Security Police units tasked with guarding American airbases in South Vietnam had been equipped only with unarmoured, machine-gun-armed M151 military utility tactical trucks. These proved unequal to the job intended and the US Air Force eventually acquired a number of M113 series APCs and a turret-less version of the US Army's M706 seen here, referred to as the XM706E2. *(Michael Green)*

In a post-Vietnam War photograph, US Air Force Security policemen are shown sprinting from an XM706E2 during a drill. In lieu of a machine-gun-armed turret, the vehicle has an open-topped parapet equipped with weapon-mounting points and gun shields. The XM706E2 first arrived in Southeast Asia in 1968. *(Defense Audio-Visual Agency)*

In a picture taken at an ARVN depot is a Second World War Two vintage Lynx scout car, a Canadian-designed and built version of the British-designed and built Daimler scout car from the same time period. The ARVN have added a small one-man open-topped turret to the vehicle. The number of such vehicles in ARVN service is unknown. Behind it is an ARVN M113 APC fitted with the turret of an American-designed and built M8 light armoured car. *(Patton Museum)*

(*Above*) Crew members of a US Army 107mm (4.2 inch) self-propelled mortar M106/M106A1 plug their ears as the weapon is about to be fired. The M30 107mm mortar first appeared in American military service in 1951 as the replacement for the older generation 107mm mortar, designated the M2, that had seen useful service during the Second World War. (*National Archives*)

(*Opposite above*) An improvised armoured car built by the ARVN of which nothing is known other than this undated photograph. Despite the large number of armoured vehicles supplied by the American Government to the ARVN, somebody must have believed there was a pressing need for something that could be locally produced. (*Patton Museum*)

(*Opposite below*) A photograph shows a US Army M30 107mm (4.2 inch) mortar mounted in either a self-propelled M106 or M106A1 mortar carrier in South Vietnam. The muzzle-loading mortar was mounted on a rotating turntable that could be turned 90 degrees and fired through a three-piece split circular hatch in the roof of the vehicle's rear hull. The vehicle had onboard storage space for eighty-eight rounds of 107mm mortar ammunition. (*Patton Museum*)

(*Above*) A factory shot of a carrier full-track mortar 81mm M125A1. There was no production authorized of the M125 model of the vehicle, based on the gasoline-engine-powered version of the M113 series of armoured personnel carriers. The 81mm mortar mounted in the M125A1 was designated the M1. It was an excellent weapon for firing on area targets. (*National Archives*)

(*Opposite page*) Looking into the interior of an 81mm self-propelled mortar M125A1 in South Vietnam, the storage racks for the mortar's ammunition is clearly visible. The six-man vehicle had authorized storage for 114 rounds of 81mm ammunition and 600 rounds for the vehicle commander's .50 calibre machine-gun. (*FMC*)

Pictured is the self-propelled flamethrower M132 or M132A1. There are no external features to distinguish between the two models of the vehicle. The small, manually operated one-man armoured turret visible on the roof contained the flame gun. Within the vehicle's passenger compartment were the fuel and pressure unit. *(TACOM)*

Shown in use during the Vietnam War is a US Army self-propelled flamethrower M132 or M132A1. The fuel tanks stored within the vehicle's passenger compartment had a capacity of 200 gallons and provided a firing time of thirty-two seconds. The flame gun had a range of between 36 feet (11m) to 656 feet (200m). *(National Archives)*

The US Army as a test deployed a small number of the relatively-new-in-service M163A1 20mm self-propelled air defence guns to South Vietnam in the ground support role. To offset the weight of the electrically-powered one-man turret fitted to the roof of the vehicle, it had flotation cells fitted to either side of the hull and a much larger trim vane fitted with a flotation cell. (*Patton Museum*)

Here we see a US Army M163A1 20mm self-propelled air defence gun exiting the water somewhere in South Vietnam. The range-only radar that was supposed to be standard equipment on these vehicles was not fitted to those sent to Southeast Asia. The M168 20mm gun on the vehicle had a rate of fire between 1,000 to 3,000 rounds per minute. (*Patton Museum*)

(*Above*) The 155mm howitzer mounted in the M109 was designated the M126 and was 14 feet 8 inches (4.51m) long. The vehicle itself with weapon pointed forward was 21 feet 8 inches (6.64m) in length and 10 feet 4 inches (3.17m) wide. Height over the turret with a .50 calibre machine-gun fitted was 10 feet 9 inches (3.32m). (*National Archives*)

(*Opposite above*) Among the many improvised weapons employed by the US Army during its time in Southeast Asia was this unarmoured M548 cargo carrier armed with an electrically-powered one-man armoured turret armed with four .50 calibre machine-guns, designated the M33. The M548 was based on the suspension system of the M113 series. (*National Archives*)

(*Opposite below*) Introduced in US Army service in the early 1960s was the 155mm self-propelled howitzer M109, two of which are seen here in South Vietnam. Protection from enemy attack for the vehicles shown here include sandbags and cyclone fencing. Both vehicles have the Type A armament sub-system vehicle commander's cupola normally seen on the M113 series APC. (*National Archives*)

(*Above*) Ready for a fire support mission in South Vietnam is a US Army 155mm self-propelled howitzer M109. It could fire a high explosive round out to a maximum range of 15,967 yards (14,600m). The standard high explosive round, designated the M107, weighed 95 pounds (43.1kg). The M109 could also fire a smoke round and an illumination round, designated the M485A2. (*National Archives*)

(*Above*) The longest range artillery piece the US Army deployed to South Vietnam was the 175mm self-propelled gun M107 seen here. The barrel on the gun was 35 feet 8 inches (10.9m) long and weighed 12,050 pounds (5,966kg). Firing a 202-pound (92kg) high explosive round, it could attain a maximum range of 35,760 yards (32,700m). (*TACOM*)

(*Opposite page, below*) Also brought to South Vietnam by the US Army was the 105mm self-propelled howitzer M108 shown here. The vehicle's 105mm howitzer was designated the M103 and had a length of 10 feet 11 inches (3.08m). The weapon could fire a 29.22 pound (15.0kg) high explosive round out to a range of 12,577 yards (11,500m). There was also an anti-personal tracer round (APERS-T) that contained 8,000 flechettes. (*National Archives*)

(*Above*) Pictured is the Rifle Multiple 106mm self-propelled M50 nicknamed the Ontos. All six of the vehicle's M40A1C 106mm recoilless rifles could be dismounted, with two of them specifically intended for that purpose. These were the top outboard rifles on either side of the vehicle and for that dismounted role were fitted with a spotting rifle and elbow telescope. (*TACOM*)

(*Opposite above*) Typically, the 175mm self-propelled gun M107, pictured here, spent most of its time in static positions at artillery fire support bases located throughout South Vietnam. To prevent any damage to the gun in transit, a large travel lock was affixed to the barrel. The spade at the rear of the vehicle was used to help absorb some of the recoil generated by the gun when fired. (*National Archives*)

(*Opposite below*) When originally designing the lightweight air transportable chassis for the 175mm self-propelled gun M107 and the 8 inch self-propelled howitzer M110, there was little thought given for the protection of the gun crew. As seen with this 8 inch self-propelled howitzer M110 in South Vietnam, the crew has added sandbags on the vehicle for a bit of extra protection. Some gun crews even added armour plate to their vehicle during the Vietnam War. (*National Archives*)

(*Above*) Running along a South Vietnamese beach is a US Marine Corps M50A1 Ontos. The gunner is manning a .30 calibre gun that could be fired from within the vehicle or operated manually by the gunner when standing in the open hatch. On the front hull of the vehicle can be seen spare band track. The band track on the Ontos was 20 inches (50.8cm) wide and divided into five sections. (*Marine Corps Historical Center*)

(*Opposite page*) The gunner aimed the six M40A1C recoilless rifles on the M50A1 Ontos through the M20A3C periscope located in the turret roof. The turret was manually operated in both traverse and elevation and could be rotated 40 degrees left or right, elevated up to 40 degrees as seen here, or depressed down to 10 degrees. (*National Archives*)

(*Above*) Accompanying a US Marine Corps infantry patrol in South Vietnam are three M50A1 Ontos. The vehicle carried eighteen main gun rounds. Besides one round carried in each of the 106mm recoilless rifles, there were eight more stored in the lower hull of the vehicle with four more rounds carried in the right rear of the crew compartment. The vehicle was 12 feet 6 inches in length (3.84m) and 8 feet 6 inches (2.62m) in width. The Ontos had a height of 6 feet 11 inches (1.86m). (*National Archives*)

(*Opposite above*) Taking part in a firing mission in South Vietnam is a US Marine Corps LVTH6 armed with a turret-mounted 105mm howitzer. The large barge-like vehicle had storage room for 151 rounds of 105mm ammunition onboard. The vehicle was 29 feet 8 inches (9.08m) in length and 11 feet 8.5 inches (3.60m) in width. Height was 13 feet 4.5 inches (4.08m). (*National Archives*)

(*Opposite below*) Based on the unarmoured amphibious cargo carrier M116 built for the US Army and the US Marine Corps, a number of lightly armoured experimental weapon armed vehicles were tested in the early 1960s, including the XM733 shown here. The US Army lost interest in the programme and cancelled it in 1966. However, the Marine Corps ordered ninety-three of them in 1966, some of which saw use during the Vietnam War. (*TACOM*)

(*Above*) One of the numerous armoured vehicles that had once belonged to the Military Vehicle Technology Foundation is this unrestored 155mm self-propelled gun M53. The vehicle was employed by the US Marine Corps during the Vietnam War and had authorized space for twenty of the 155mm rounds. Beginning in 1956, the US Army began rearming all of its M53s with 8-inch howitzers. (*Michael Green*)

(*Opposite above*) The 8-inch self-propelled howitzer M55 seen here was identical to the 155mm self-propelled gun M53 and employed the same mount for the two different weapons. The only difference between the two vehicles was the ammunition storage arrangement. When configured as the M55, the vehicle could only carry ten of the larger 8-inch rounds. As with the M53, the US Marine Corps used the M55 during the early years of its time in Southeast Asia. The 8-inch howitzer on the M55 had a maximum range of 16,008 yards (14,638m). (*Michael Green*)

(*Opposite below*) One of the most unusual armoured vehicles brought to South Vietnam by the Australian Army was the M113A1 Fire Support Vehicle seen here. It consisted of the M113A1 APC modified to mount the 76mm main gun armed turret from a British-designed and built armoured car named the Saladin, which the Australian Army had acquired in small numbers in the early 1960s. (*FMC*)

(*Above*) Supplied to the ARVN by the American military along with the M113 APC in the early 1960s was the command and reconnaissance vehicle M114 seen here. This particular restored example belongs to the Virginia Museum of Military Vehicles. The vehicle had a length of 14 feet 7.75 inches (4.48m) and a width of 7 feet 7.75 inches (2.35m). With a roof-mounted .50 calibre machine-gun fitted, the vehicle had a height of 7 feet 10 inches (2.16m). (*Michael Green*)

(*Opposite above*) In the foreground we see an ARVN-manned command and reconnaissance vehicle M114, while in the background is an ARVN-manned M113 APC. Operational use of the M114 in South Vietnam showed that it lacked the off-road mobility of the M113 and due to the design of the vehicle's front hull had a difficult time entering and leaving waterways. (*National Archives*)

(*Opposite below*) Despite its poor showing during its brief tenure in South Vietnam, the US Army continued to work on improving the command and reconnaissance vehicle M114. The follow-on version of the M114 was the M114A1. Pictured is the interior of an M114A1. There were 619 units of the M114 constructed for the US Army and 3,905 units of the M114A1. (*Chris Hughes*)

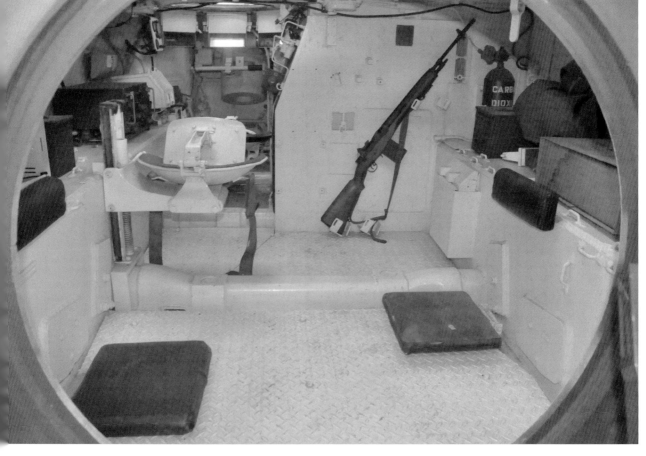

On display at the former US Army Ordnance Museum is an SU-76M tank destroyer captured from the Chinese Army during the Korean War. The NVA supposedly received the SU-76M along with the first shipment of T-34-85 medium tanks in 1959 from the Soviet Union. There is no pictorial evidence of its use in combat and one can only assume it was reserved for training duties only. *(Michael Green)*

The SU-100 tank destroyer pictured formerly resided on display at the US Army Ordnance Museum, as seen here. It is unclear if this type of vehicle was ever used by the NVA in combat. It may have only been employed as a training vehicle. When first introduced into Red Army service in the Second World War it was intended to deal with the German introduction of the Tiger B heavy tank. *(Michael Green)*

On display at the Israeli Tank Museum at Latrun is a captured Russian-designed and built ZSU-57-2. The vehicle is 27 feet (8.4m) in length and 10 feet (3.2m) in width. It has a height of 9 feet (2.7m). The 57mm guns on the ZSU-57-2 have a realistic horizontal range of 2.5 miles (4km) and a realistic vertical ceiling of 14,750 feet (4.5km). *(Vladimir Yakubov)*

Pictured is a Russian-designed and built ZSU-23-4 in the markings of the former East German Army with four liquid-cooled 23mm cannons. Notice the antenna for the RPK-2 Tobol radar at the rear roof of the turret, which has a detection range of 12 miles (20km). The NATO designation for the RPK-2 Tobol is Gun Dish. *(Michael Green)*

Being employed by the US Marine Corps during a training exercise is a captured Russian-designed and built ZSU-23-4. Obsolete by modern air defence standards, the ZSU-23-4 has been replaced by more modern air defence vehicles in the Russian Army. *(Defense Audio Visual Center)*

On display for many years at the former US Army Ordnance Museum is this improvised antiaircraft vehicle constructed by the NVA upon the chassis of a Russian-designed and built T-34-85 medium tank. The open-topped turret features twin 37mm Chinese-built air-cooled antiaircraft guns. The vehicle was captured by the ARVN in 1972 and turned over to the US Army for technical study. *(Michael Green)*

Chapter Four

Armoured Support Vehicles

There were no M60 series main battle tanks employed by the US Army during the Vietnam War as there was no need for its more powerful 105mm main gun. There were, however, a couple of variants of the vehicle that saw service during the conflict. One of these was the M728 combat engineer vehicle (CEV) based on the chassis of the M60A1 main battle tank. Weighing 115,000lb (52mt), the four-man vehicle was powered by a diesel engine that gave it a top speed of 30mph (48km/h) and an approximate operational range of 280 miles (450km) on level roads.

The M728 was armed with a 165mm demolition main gun firing rounds optimized for breaching concrete obstacles. There was space inside the vehicle for the stowage of thirty main gun rounds. The engineer equipment on the M728 included an 'A' frame boom with a lifting capacity of 17,500lb (8mt), a winch with a towing capacity of 25,000lb (11mt) and the M9 bulldozer blade. The vehicle retained the roof mounted .50 calibre machine-gun and the 7.62mm coaxial machine-gun from the M60A1 main battle tank. The maximum armour thickness on the vehicle's front hull was 143mm.

The usefulness of the M728 appears in this quote from a 1974 US Army publication entitled *Vietnam Studies: Tactical and Material Innovations*:

> In the 23d Infantry Division (Americal) the combat engineer vehicle repeatedly proved to be a valuable asset to engineer and infantry operations. The vehicle was used in fire support, base security, counter-ambush fire, direct assault of fortified positions, and limited reconnaissance by fire. It even spearheaded an infantry-cavalry charge in the village of Tap An Bac on 19 June 1969, when division elements came to the defense of two bulldozers and a work party from the 26th Engineer Battalion. The day-long fight was won in the final assault.

Deployed to South Vietnam by the US Army were the gasoline engine powered M48A2C armoured vehicle launched bridge (AVLB) and the diesel engine powered M60A1 AVLB. These turretless, two-man vehicles had no weapons. Their only job was to launch and recover their 60 foot (18.3m) hydraulically-operated aluminium alloy scissor-type bridges over obstacles. The M48A2C AVLB weighed 126,000lb (57mt) and the M60A1 AVLB weighed 122,000lb (55mt) with their bridges mounted. In a secondary role, the power and traction of the AVLBs made them an excellent tank retriever when the M88 armoured recovery vehicle was not available.

From an operational report by the 1st Battalion, 69th Armor, 3d Brigade Task Force, 25th Infantry Division dated February 15, 1967 comes this extract regarding the use of the M48A2C AVLB in South Vietnam:

> The AVLB has been used on numerous occasions to permit rapid crossing of obstacles. It extended the use of Route 19 to Duc Co for a period of a month after the ford at YA975291 became unusable. During Operation Circle Pines the AVLB was used to allow the battalion entry and exit of the area of operation … The M48 version of the AVLB is obsolete, too heavy and subject to mechanical failure but the system is an absolute requirement for armor units.

US Army armoured recovery vehicles

To assist in the recovery and repair of its armoured vehicle fleet, the US Army deployed the M88 armoured recovery vehicle (ARV) to South Vietnam, which incorporated components from the M48 series medium tank. The four-man vehicle weighed approximately 110,000lb (50mt) and was powered by a gasoline engine that provided it with a top speed of level roads of 30mph (48km/h). The maximum operational range of the M88 on roads was approximately 200 miles (322km).

The M88 was fitted with a main winch with a capacity of 90,000lb (41mt) and a lifting boom with a capacity of 50,000lb (23mt). For self-defence, the vehicle was fitted with a single, roof-mounted .50 calibre machine-gun and was authorized to carry within the vehicle's crew compartment a shoulder-fired antitank weapon. The maximum armour thickness on the front of the M88 was 38mm. Production of a diesel engine powered version of the M88 did not begin until 1975. The introduction of the new engine resulted in the vehicle being re-designated as the M88A1.

Another specialized recovery vehicle that made it to South Vietnam with the US Army was the light recovery vehicle M578. The three-man vehicle was equipped with 30,000lb (14mt) capacity boom line winch and 60,000lb (27mt) capacity tow winch. The M578 weighed 54,000lb (24mt) and was powered by a diesel engine that gave it a top speed on level roads of 37mph (60km/h) and an approximate operational range of 450 miles (724km) on level roads. For self-defence, the vehicle was fitted with a single roof-mounted .50 calibre machine-gun. Armour protection at the front of the vehicle was 13mm thick.

US Army M113 armoured support vehicles

Despite the amphibious capabilities of the M113 series, a need developed for an AVLB based on its chassis. A 33-foot (10m) aluminium alloy scissor-type bridge was developed by the US Army Mobility Equipment Research and Development Center at Fort Belvoir that could be carried and launched by an M113. The portable bridge weighed 2,700lb (1.22mt) and could support a 30,000lb (14mt) load when deployed. The vehicle with bridge launcher unit was referred to as the Marginal Terrain Assault Bridge.

There was a command post carrier version of the M113 series deployed to South Vietnam by the US Army designated as the M577, and was easily identified by its high, box-like silhouette that covered the vehicle's rear passenger compartment. This allowed those within to stand up, which was not possible in the other versions of the M113 series. There was also a tent extension that could be attached to the rear of the vehicle's hull to provide an additional work area. A diesel engine powered version of the M577 became the M577A1.

Prior to the introduction of the M577/M577A1 into the Vietnam War, US Army and ARVN units used a modified M113/M113A1 in that role. As the addition of three large antennas to the modified M113/M113A1 command vehicles clearly identified them as important targets to the VC or NVA, the crews were instructed to vary their locations while moving in formation to make it harder for the enemy to predict their position at any given time for targeted destruction.

Marine Corps armoured support vehicles

Deployed to South Vietnam by the US Marine Corps was a command version of the LVTP5, designated as the LVTP5 (CMD). It was manned by a crew of ten men with six being radio operators. Inside the vehicle there was room for nine radios divided between two racks.

In addition to the LVTP5 (CMD), the Marine Corps employed a maintenance and recovery version of the LVTP5, known as the LVTR1 in South Vietnam. It was fitted with a 60,000lb (27mt) capacity winch on the front of the vehicle's roof that was used to install or remove power-packs (engine/transmission units) from other versions of the LVTP5 family of vehicles, or other heavy objects. There was also an engineer version, designated the LVTE1, that mounted a large, fearsome looking excavator on the front hull deployed to South Vietnam and could fire the M125 line charge to clear mines.

An ARV employed by the US Marine Corps during the Vietnam War in place of the US Army's M88 ARV was the heavy recovery vehicle M51. Based on components from the M103 heavy tank, which would not see service during the Vietnam War, the M51 had a 60,000lb (27mt) capacity crane and a 90,000lb (41mt) capacity main winch. There was also a 10,000lb (5mt) capacity auxiliary winch. Entering into production for the US Marine Corps and US Army in 1954, the four-man vehicle weighed 120,000lb (54mt).

Powered by a gasoline engine, the M51 had a top speed on level roads of 30mph (48km/h) and an approximate operational range of 150 miles (241km). For self-defence, the vehicle was fitted with a single, roof-mounted .50 calibre machine-gun. Maximum armour protection at the front of the vehicle was 38mm thick. Like all the ARVs employed by the American military in South Vietnam, it was considered a prime target by the enemy as it could be used to return damaged and destroyed tanks and armoured fighting vehicles to service.

Allied armoured support vehicles

For their tanks and armoured fighting vehicles deployed to South Vietnam, the Australian Army sent along the four-man Centurion Armoured Recovery Vehicle Mk 2. The 99,207lb (45mt) vehicle first entered British Army service in 1956. Unlike the American M88, the Centurion Armoured Recovery Vehicle Mk 2 lacked a recovery boom. The Australian Army also deployed to South Vietnam a variant of the M113A1, referred to as a fitter's vehicle that was equipped with a 6,800lb (3.1mt) capacity winch on the vehicle's roof. The crane could be used to lift out and replace such items as vehicle power packs. This variant never entered in US Army service as the M88 and M578 performed the same role.

The Australian Army did bring with them a couple of Centurion tank-based bridge launchers to South Vietnam. They were known as the Centurion Mk 5 bridge-layer and could launch a 52-foot-long one-piece steel bridge when called upon. They also brought two Centurion Mk 5 tank-dozers.

Pictured is the full-tracked combat engineer vehicle M728 as employed by the US Army during the Vietnam War. It was armed with a 165mm main gun, designated the M135 that fired a 67.6 pound (30.7kg) high explosive squash head (HESH) round, originally intended for the destruction of concrete obstacles. (*TACOM*)

Mounted on the top of the 165mm main gun on the M728 was a 2.2kw xenon searchlight capable of generating white or infra-red light. The 165mm main gun on the vehicle had a maximum rate of fire of only two rounds per minute. The muzzle velocity of the rounds fired from the vehicle's main gun was 850ft/sec (259m/sec). (TACOM)

The turret on a US Army full-tracked combat engineer vehicle M728 has been reversed on the vehicle pictured. Projecting out from the rear of the turret is its A frame lifting boom, shown in its stored position. The vehicle had storage space for thirty 165mm main gun rounds and 600 rounds of .50 calibre ammunition. (TACOM)

(*Above*) An overhead photograph of an armoured vehicle launched bridge (AVLB) based on the modified chassis of the M60A1 main battle tank. The vehicle had a two-man crew with the driver's position located on the left side of the hull and the vehicle commander's position located on the right side of the hull. (*TACOM*)

(*Opposite above*) Taken in South Vietnam is this photograph of an armoured vehicle launched bridge (AVLB) without the bridge. The chassis is that of an M48A2C medium tank, as is evident from the elliptically shaped front hull. When work began on an AVLB, the chassis chosen was the M46 medium tank. By the time the bridge design was finalized it was mounted on the chassis of the newer medium tank M48A2C. (*National Archives*)

(*Opposite below*) Shown in South Vietnam is an armoured vehicle launched bridge (AVLB) based on the modified chassis of the M60A1 main battle tank, the replacement for the M48A2C chassis. The stunted vegetation visible in the photograph indicates that the area has likely been sprayed with chemical defoliants to deny the enemy cover from which to ambush American military units. (*National Archives*)

The controls for operating the 60-foot (18.3m) hydraulically-operated aluminium alloy scissor-type bridge seen here on the modified chassis of the M60A1 main battle tank were located in front of the driver's position. The American military acquired 401 units of the AVLB on the M60A1 chassis between 1964 and 1981. *(TACOM)*

Employed in South Vietnam by the US Army was the medium recovery vehicle M88 seen here. A total of 1,075 units of the vehicle were built between 1960 and 1964. The vehicle was powered by a gasoline engine designated the AVSI-1790-6A, the most powerful in the US Army's inventory at the time. The engine was coupled to the Allison XT-1400-2 transmission with three gears forward and one in reverse. *(TACOM)*

Crossing a stream in South Vietnam is this M88. The vehicle had a four-man crew consisting of the vehicle commander, driver, mechanic and rigger for the hoisting boom. The vehicle's driver and mechanic were located at the front of the vehicle with the driver on the left-hand side of the hull. The vehicle commander's cupola was located in the centre of the roof with the rigger riding inside the vehicle. *(TACOM)*

(*Above*) Employed in South Vietnam by the US Army was the light recovery vehicle M578 shown here. It rode on the same chassis as the 175mm self-propelled gun M107 and the 8 inch self-propelled howitzer M110. The M578 had a three-man crew and the armoured turret with its lifting boom could be traversed 360 degrees. It also had two winches, with a 30,000lb and 60,000lb capacity. (*TACOM*)

(*Opposite above*) Here we see the A frame lifting boom of the US Army medium recovery vehicle M88 being used to hold a 155mm self-propelled howitzer M109. The M88 was 27 feet 1.5 inches (8.26m) long and 11 feet 3 inches (3.44m) wide. To the top of the roof-mounted .50 calibre machine-gun the M88 was 10 feet 7 inches (3.3m) in height. (*TACOM*)

(*Opposite below*) Working in tandem, two US Army medium recovery vehicle M88s in South Vietnam are being used to load a badly damaged M48A3 medium tank onto a flatbed trailer. The M88 rode on a torsion bar suspension system and road wheels inherited from the M48 series of medium tanks. (*National Archives*)

(*Above*) Shown in South Vietnam is this light recovery vehicle M578 being employed to transport large coils of concertina wire. There is a hydraulically operated spade at the rear of the vehicle. The vehicle is 20 feet 10 inches (6.13m) long and 10 feet 4 inches (3.17m) wide. With a roof-mounted .50 calibre machine-gun fitted it is 10 feet 10.5 inches (3.08m) tall. (*National Archives*)

(*Opposite above*) The prototype of the Marginal Terrain Assault Bridge is shown being tested in a body of water. The test was done to confirm that, despite the additional weight imposed by the 33 foot (10m) bridge mounted on the roof of the M113 series vehicle, the M113 retained its amphibious characteristics. (*TACOM*)

(*Opposite below*) Prior to the introduction of the Marginal Terrain Assault Bridge on the M113 to South Vietnam by the US Army, the ARVN came up with an improvised bridging system mounted on the front of their M113 APCs. It is unclear if this was intended only for use by personnel or could be adapted to allow light vehicles to cross. (*National Archives*)

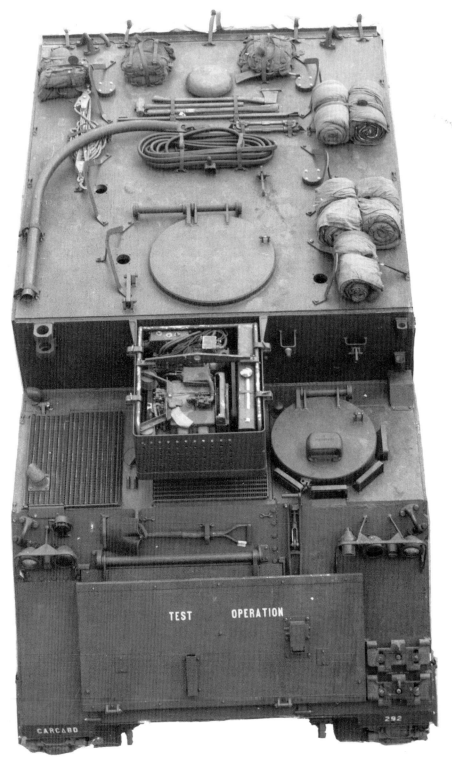

An overhead view of the M577 command post-carrier showing the auxiliary gasoline-powered generator mounted on the outside front wall of the passenger compartment. The generator could be removed from the vehicle and placed on the ground by the lifting davit seen lying flat on the roof of the passenger compartment. During ground operations the generator provided electrical power to the vehicle by way of a 50 foot (15.24m) cable. (TACOM)

If required, the large tent normally stored on the rear roof of the M577 command post carrier's passenger compartment could be joined together with the tent of another M577, as seen here. The height of the passenger compartment on the M577 was raised 25.25 inches (64cm), providing headroom inside the vehicle's rear passenger compartment of 6 feet 2.75 inches (1.9m). (FMC)

A rear view of a M577 command post carrier. A generator at the front of the vehicle's raised superstructure provided power for the onboard radios and lights when the vehicle's engine was turned off. The generator could be removed from the vehicle and placed on the ground and connected by way of a 50-foot (15.24m) cable. (FMC)

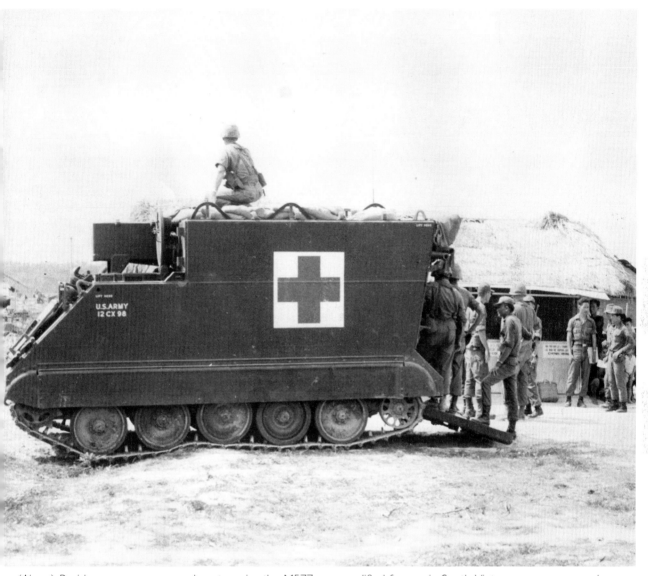

(*Above*) Besides use as a command post-carrier the M577 was modified for use in South Vietnam as an armoured ambulance, as seen here. The American military had over 300,000 men wounded during the conflict in Southeast Asia. Of these approximately 10,000 lost at least one limb. Due to the efficiency of the medical facilities employed during the Vietnam War, 82 per cent of the seriously wounded American military personnel survived their injuries. (*National Archives*)

(*Opposite above*) This picture was taken inside the erected tent stored on the rear roof of the M577 command post carrier's passenger compartment. In the foreground a soldier is seen talking on a portable telephone switchboard. In the background can be seen another soldier inside the vehicle's passenger compartment. (*National Archives*)

(*Opposite below*) On the front of this M577 or M577A1 command post-carrier shown here in South Vietnam are two strands of concertina wire. The vehicle commander on the M577 had an overhead hatch but there were no provisions for mounting a .50 calibre machine-gun on the roof of the vehicle. Inside the vehicle's passenger compartment was a folding table and provisions for a large map board. (*National Archives*)

Because there was limited space for the storage of fuel inside the rear passenger compartment of the M113-series, the firing duration of the self-propelled flamethrower M132 and M132A1 was relatively short. The US Army had a small number of M548 cargo carriers armoured, becoming the XM45E1 flamethrower service vehicle seen here, to refuel the flame thrower vehicle. *(FMC)*

Being used to remove the power train from a US Marine Corps LVTP5 in South Vietnam is the maintenance and recovery version of the vehicle, designated the LVTR1. The vehicle had a large lifting boom located on the roof at the very front of the hull. The LVTR1 was also equipped with welding equipment and an air compressor. *(National Archives)*

On display at the Camp Pendleton Marine Corps base in Southern California is an example of the LVTE1. It was an engineering version of the LVTP5 intended to breach minefields with its massive front hull-mounted excavator blade. It was also able to launch line charges for breaching minefields from the large bracket seen on the roof of the vehicle.
(Paul Hannah)

Two Marine Corps LVTE1s are seen on the move during the Vietnam War. The large steel and aluminium excavator blade located at the front of the vehicle's hull weighed 10,000 pounds (4535kg.) To maintain the vehicle's trim in water, flotation tanks were fitted behind the excavator blades. The LVTE1 weighed 94,470 pounds (42mt).
(National Archives)

Employed by the Marine Corps during the Vietnam War was the heavy recovery vehicle M51 shown here. The design study for the vehicle began in 1951 and the first pilot vehicles showed up at the Aberdeen Proving Ground for testing in 1953. Production of the vehicle began in 1954 and ended the following year with 187 units completed. (TACOM)

Another view of the heavy recovery vehicle M51 showing the large crane and the rear spade. The cab at the front of the vehicle housed the four-man crew consisting of the vehicle commander, driver, crane operator and rigger. The vehicle was 33 feet 3 inches in length (10.13m) and 11 feet 11 inches in width. With a roof-mounted .50 calibre machine-gun fitted it was 10 feet 9 inches (3.28m) in height. (TACOM)

Seen here on display at the Israeli Tank Museum at Lantrun is a British-designed and built Centurion Armoured Recovery Vehicle Mk 2. This vehicle was employed by the Australian Army to support its Centurion tanks during their time in the Vietnam War. The vehicle is 29 feet 9 inches (8.87m) in length and 11 feet 11.5 inches (3.39m) in width. Vehicle height is 9 feet 6 inches (2.83m). *(Vladimir Yakubov)*

On display at Fort Leonard Wood, Missouri, is this captured Russian-designed and built MTU-20 bridging tank. Both ends of the cantilever bridge mounted on the T-54/T-55 medium tank chassis are folded over the structure for ease of transporting. When ready to emplace, the ends of the bridges are folded down and the entire structure is then pushed forward by a hydraulically-operated mechanism until an obstacle is crossed. *(Loren Hannah)*

As the Australian Army did not acquire the light recovery vehicle M578 or the medium recovery vehicle M88, it depended on a modified version of the M113A1, known as a fitter's vehicle, to service its own fleet of light vehicles. The fitter's vehicle, as seen here, was operated by two men and mounted a large crane. *(FMC)*

Notes

Notes

Notes

Notes

Notes

Notes